Volume 2 Issue 3 September 2015

CW00508516

Contents

From the Editor

Welcome to our First Anniversary Edition.

We have been blown away by your feedback so far with readers descriptions detailing that they feel personally empowered and supported just by being a subscriber and that they feel our subject matter is 'Inspirational'.

Thank you so much for your feedback, we will as always endeavour to keep you all informed.

Many thanks for reading. Liz

N.B. Natural products and holistic services should not be considered a substitute for veterinary treatment. If you suspect your animal is ill, please take them to your nearest veterinary surgeon as soon as possible.

is a family owned company

Sponsored by

Published by

Copyright © Healthful 2011 - 2015

Editor: Liz Roberts   Photo Editor: John Fieldsend   Advertising Manager: Nick Harding

 Facebook.com/HealthfulDog

Plus.google.com/+HealthfulUKDogs

www.youtube.com/c/HealthfulUKDogs

 twitter.com/HealthfulDog

healthfuldog.tumblr.com

facebook.com/HealthfulAloe

 pinterest.com/healthfuldog

instagram.com/healthful_dog

healthfuldog.podbean.com

Animal Matters

Communication is the key to all healing

Animal Matters

Elaine Downs

AN ANIMAL COMMUNICATORS' TAKE ON WHY ANIMALS APPEAR TO MISBEHAVE SOMETIMES

I want to start my article this time by posing a question to all our readers.

"How many of you have sometimes taken your animals' unwanted behaviour as a sign that they are being disobedient, disrespectful, or even the dreaded "D" word, dominant!! ??"

It's okay if you have I am not here to judge you. I just want to give you some other options to consider.

What Sue and I have discovered from conducting many hundreds of communications with animals over the years, is that there are many other reasons for animals behaving in a way we would rather they didn't.

In fact Sue had an experience of this sort of unwanted behaviour from her Jack Russell Terrier, Sally, many years ago, not long after she had adopted her from a rescue centre.

Sally was on the sofa one day and growled at Sue when she asked her to get down. Sue said "I thought this was very out of character for Sally, but, at that time I felt that she was trying to challenge my authority, so, I made her get off the sofa and sent her out into the garden, still growling at me. I remember saying to Sally, "Don't you dare growl at me." Later that day Sue took Sally to her vet as this incident kept nagging at her. Sue's vet examined Sally, and as he squeezed one of her teats, a jet of milk squirted out. Sue felt terrible. The reason that Sally had growled at her was because she was having a phantom pregnancy, and was protecting the puppies that she thought she was carrying in her womb. She wasn't trying to challenge Sue's authority at all."

Sue had jumped to a conclusion about the reason for Sally's behaviour that day and had got it very wrong.

We had the pleasure of working with a beautiful Springer Spaniel called Daisy some years ago. Daisy's human Mum and Dad came to us because they couldn't work out what to do about Daisy's behaviour

She appeared to be very depressed and had stopped playing with her Springer Spaniel sister Nell, wasn't coming back to her people on walks when she was called, and was being growly with other dogs on walks too.

It transpired that she was upset because she felt that her human guardians were not giving her choices, and not considering her in their decisions around the two dogs. Both dogs slept outside at night, and Daisy wanted the choice to sleep inside when she wanted to. Also she had been spayed and was very upset about having the option to have puppies taken away from her without being consulted. She was very sad about everything and felt she wasn't valued.

Sue and I communicated with Daisy once and we also gave her a Bodytalk session. When her human Mum rang us a couple of weeks later to give us feedback on Daisy, this is what she said: "On walks, Daisy behaved much better and we didn't have to keep shouting at her to come back. She started to play again with our other Springer and with us and she also wanted to be with us more. Overall, she is a much happier girl and has got her lovely playfulness back."

We also had the pleasure of communicating with a beautiful Palomino horse called Mylo. Mylo had a habit of biting people when they got too close to him. He was very angry and upset, and was taking it out on anybody who got too close, particularly his human guardian Jacci. She had lots of bruises from his teeth.

Jacci told us that he and some of the other stallions on the yard were castrated round about the same time. She said that the other two horses calmed down quite quickly after their castration. However, Mylo had not changed a bit, his behaviour was just as bad.

When he was communicated with, he told us how very upset and angry he was at being castrated, and how when he was entire he was a proud stallion, but now he felt that all his power and majesty had been taken from him without permission. He also felt that he couldn't trust Jacci anymore because of this. He felt very sad that, from his perspective, Jacci had destroyed the trust they had between them. Also he felt that she just expected him to do things without any negotiation, and because he felt the trust had been damaged he didn't see why he should do anything that she said.

We explained to him that Jacci had only done what she felt was best for him, because when he was a stallion his behaviour was quite aggressive and that made him unsafe. Jacci told us that when he was a colt, he was in a field with two very aggressive stallions. Mylo said he thought that was how to behave as a stallion, because that is what the other two horses had shown him.

Sue and I worked with Mylo visiting him at his stables once a week for a few weeks. We used communication combined with Bodytalk, and we are glad to report that he is now much softer and has released his feelings of anger and sadness. He now understands that he is a wonderful, powerful, proud horse exactly as he is. Also, Jacci now negotiates with him and he feels listened to. The best part is he has stopped biting people. He still brushes you with his teeth sometimes, but his jaws are firmly closed, and that action is more of reassurance behaviour now.

I have used these three examples to show how we get it wrong with our animals from time to time. There are many reasons why our animals may behave in what we regard as an inappropriate manner from time to time. They may be feeling ill, upset with us or another animal in the household. They may be busy doing something that is important to them, may be in pain, or be uncomfortable because they are wearing ill fitting equipment. We shouldn't always expect our animals to jump to it the minute we want something. Respect their space and ask them what is wrong if they are displaying unusual behaviours. Don't immediately jump to conclusions, because quite often those conclusions can be wrong, and you may be setting yourself or your animal up to fail.

Until next time. Enjoy what's left of your summer with your beloved animals.

Elaine and Sue

"ANIMAL MATTERS": www.animalcommunication.co.uk
TEL: 01937 580854   MOBILES:- Elaine: 07976 889979   Sue: 07973 622202
FACEBOOK: http://www.facebook.com/pages/Animal-Communication/78523923007

Bardic the Newshound

The Dog Welfare Alliance is a non-profit organization that connects all those who have an interest in dog behavior and welfare. Your memberships/ subscriptions and donations are passed on to rescue shelters so that they can save dogs in urgent need and ultimately, as the organization grows, these will also fund education programs and dog sanctuaries. Numerous dogs have had their rescue and veterinary costs funded by the DWA in the short time since it launched.

http://www.dogwelfarealliance.com/

Events:

Energy Healing 1 or 2 day Workshop Catherine O'Driscoll 10:00-17:00 5th & 6th September Kingston Lisle Village Hall, nr Wantage £50 first day £95 for both Sarah-Jane 07753 856446	**The Truth About Wolves and Dogs** Toni Shelbourne 9:30—16:30 Saturday 12th September 2015 Best Behaviour 3 Holmes St, Rossendale, Lancs. £55—Book via: http://www.bestbehaviouranimaltherapy.co.uk/page26.htm
Holistic Canine Healthcare Catherine O'Driscoll 09:00—16:00 Saturday 12th September 2015 Raystede Centre for Animal Welfare, Lewes Book via: Sally Cronk 01435 867484	**Discover Dogs** Adults £16, Concessions £13 (cheaper if booked in advance) 10:00—17:00 17th & 18thOctober 2015 Excel London www.discoverdogs.org.uk
All About Dogs 9:30—17:00 17th& 18th October 2015 Newark Showground Adults £9 Children £5 www.allaboutdogsshow.co.uk	**A Weekend of Obedience Training** Mary Ray 31st October & 1st November 2015 Moreton Community Centre, Maryland Ave, Moreton, Cheshire £70 handlers, £35 Spectators julierowlands@sky.com 07983 716685

Book Review

The Aromatic Dog

Nayana Morag

In this book we are gently introduced to the history and reasoning for zoopharacognosy and how important it is to approach any issue holistically.

The explanation of choices of oils or hydrosols in particular situations is very clear and the illustrations are charming, especially as the author has made it clear that the photographs are of her own dog.

There are detailed instructions of how to make up gels, hydrosols and other forms of aromatics with details of when and where to use them.

The book includes a comprehensive list of essential oils, hydrosols and even the herbal and carrier oils needed, their history and when they can be useful, but it is stressed that it is important that the dog makes the final decision on which is to be used. There is a very handy cross reference chart and a great list of what aromatics are recommended for specific conditions.

Overall this book appears to be both a great introduction to a powerful holistic healing modality as well as a fantastic reference manual for putting it into practice.

For regular articles on Zoopharmacognosy see our fantastic section written by Karen Webb of Let Your Animal Lead (this edition page 148).

Felines in Focus—You feed your cat *what*?

Tracy Dion

As a feline writer, consultant and website founder – i.e., someone truly passionate about improving feline care – I talk to a lot of cat owners. And for all the years I've been in this field, I'm still surprised when I meet someone for the first time and learn their families eat local organic, their dogs eat raw, and their cat eats dry kibble.

And every time, I have to bit my lip to keep from snapping, *"Your cat eats what?"*

You love your dogs, you've done the research and you know a menu of fresh, species-appropriate meat-based meals is the most nutritious, easily digestible diet you can offer them. Likewise, you and your human family members will benefit most by a diet based primarily on fresh fruits and vegetables. The cat, however, continues to get short shrift via that bag of dry, highly processed kibble with, perhaps, an occasional can of moist food thrown in for good measure.

It's time to change that.

Under unfavorable conditions when meat is scarce, wolves and dogs will snack on berries and roots. Their digestive systems are capable of breaking down the plant material and extracting enough nutrition from it to make the eating worthwhile, if not optimal. Cats, however, have a much more limited ability to effectively process plant material and cannot extract everything they need to live – much less flourish – on fruits, vegetables or grains.

Although both dogs and cats fall under the order "Carnivora" and both naturally do well on a balanced diet of raw meat, bones and organs, cats are "obligate" carnivores, meaning they don't just prosper on such a diet, they require it. As amazing as the

improvements seen with dogs transitioned to raw, the improvements seen in feline health and vitality when cats are fed what their bodies are so beautifully designed to process is nothing short of breathtaking.

Proper nutrition is the building block upon which health is built for all living creatures, and this applies doubly so to cats, with their sharply defined dietary needs. Like birds of prey, snakes and other obligate carnivores, cats are designed inside and out to catch and eat whole prey. Every aspect of feline physiology demonstrates that obtaining what it needs to achieve optimum health – not just survive but truly thrive – depends upon fulfilling its fresh, prey-based dietary requirements.

From their sharp eyesight, keen hearing and fearsome claws and teeth, to their exceptional stalking, pouncing and sprinting abilities, the cat's body is built to hunt. Apex predators in nearly every environment they occupy, they are one of nature's most perfectly designed killing machines.

They are so well designed, in fact, there has been virtually no genetic drift in the 10,000 years since the African Wild Cat ancestors of today's housecats were brought out of the Middle Eastern deserts. That tabby purring so contentedly on your lap is virtually indistinguishable, at the genetic level, from today's African Wild Cat (1).

As efficient a predator as they are outwardly, the cat's digestive physiol-

ogy is even more specialized around its prey-based dietary needs.

Starting at the very basic digestive level, a meal that includes large amounts of animal protein causes an increased flow of saliva, as well as production of the most effective combination of digestive enzymes in that saliva. Similarly, the stomach, gall bladder, pancreas, and upper and lower intestines all secrete a mix of enzymes that are positively responsive to the presence of large amounts of animal protein, ensuring a high level of digestive efficacy throughout the entire digestive tract. Animal tissues, bones and organs are chemically broken down and assimilated at an extremely high level of efficiency and thoroughness, providing the cat with maximal nutrients while expending minimal energy (2). Cats fed standard commercial diets must expend more energy to digest their foods less thoroughly, and do not enjoy the smaller and less frequent stools of raw-fed cats.

Furthermore, unlike dogs, cats are metabolically adapted for preferential use of animal protein and fat as energy sources, and they require a certain minimum of animal protein to fuel the most basic bodily functions. This minimum protein requirement is hard-wired and if the diet does not contain enough for their daily needs, or they are unable to process an adequate

amount due to low bio-availability, cats will sabotage the muscles in their own bodies to obtain their daily needs (3). (This is part of the reason muscle wasting is so prevalent among senior kitties.)

Comparatively-speaking, cats require a fairly high level of fat in their diet – about 20% – and that, too, is thoroughly and efficiently utilized. You will seldom encounter an overweight cat on a balanced raw diet (4).

In addition, several nutrients are found abundantly in the bodies of their prey and cats – unlike most animals including, in some cases, dogs – are unable to synthesize them and must get their daily requirements from their diet, including:

• Eleven different amino acids: arginine (both), histidine (both), isoleucine (both), leucine (both), lysine (both), methionine (both), phenylalanine (both), threonine (both), tyrptophan (both), valine (both), and, of course, taurine (cats only).

• Vitamins A (cats only) and D (both).

• Niacin. Dogs can create all the Niacin they need. Cats can create this to some degree, but the amount is insufficient to their needs.

• The fatty acid Arachadonic. Dogs can make their own from certain fats. Cats cannot.

Sadly, many standard commercial diets do not contain enough fresh, bio-available protein to fulfil a cat's daily requirement. Although raw feeding is

becoming increasingly more accepted, over 98% of today's housecats are still fed these commercial diets, primarily kibble, and quite often on a free-feeding schedule. Kibble is a singularly inappropriate "food" product for cats. Because of the very nature of their manufacture, kibble requires some form of carbohydrate content. Many of them are loaded with grains, while others have substituted potatoes or another starch; seemingly more benign, but in reality still a "food" the cat's body is ill-equipped to process.

Cats have no dietary need for carbohydrates and have either lost or never had some of the enzymatic pathways needed to process them. Without those pathways for energy conversion, carbs are processed and stored as fat. Worst of all, being forced to process such a foreign diet stresses the cat's body enormously and reduces protein absorption (5). That, combined with a chronically dehydrated state of being – as desert animal descendants, cats have a low thirst drive and an inefficient method of drinking water (their lapping mechanics are not the same as a dog's) – and kibble is potentially the single largest underlying cause of many of the diseases and other illnesses sweeping in epidemic proportions across our domestic cat populations. Obesity, diabetes, urinary tract issues, inflammatory bowel disease (often a precursor for intestinal cancer, or lymphoma), kidney disease, allergies, vomiting and diarrhea are just a few of the ailments that have been linked in some manner to kibble-laden diets.

Conclusion

As healthy as a meat-based diet is for our dogs, it is doubly so for our cats. Evolution, science and logic all point to

a fresh raw prey-based diet as being the most appropriate, nutritious, and easily-digestible diet for today's carnivorous pets, and anecdotal evidence is overwhelmingly in favor of raw diets. With the increased scrutiny being given to what America's pet owners feed their furry family members, it's easy to foresee a time when they will consider feeding raw products to cats and dogs as common-sense healthy as we do giving whole, fresh foods to our kids. Not everyone eats or serves whole apples over the fast-food apple Danish, but there is no doubt in our minds which of the two is healthier.

So the next time you toss down a rabbit for your dogs, maybe drop a mouse or a chick to satisfy and nourish the carnivore in your kitty. ;-)

References

1. Carlos A. Drisco, et. al, (June, 2007), *The Near Eastern Origin of Cat Domestication*, Science Express

2. National Research Council (U.S.), (2006), *The Nutrient requirements of dogs and cats*, National Research Council Ad Hoc Committee on Dog and Cat Nutrition, Chapter One

3. Mark A. Peterson, DVM, (December, 2011), *Can Increasing the Amount of Fat or Carbohydrate in a Cat's Diet Compensate for Low Protein Intake?*, Insights into Veterinarian Endocrinology

4. Debra Zoran (12/2002), *The carnivore connection to nutrition in cats*, originally published in the Journal of the American Veterinary Medical Association (AVMA)

5. Karen Becker, DVM (05/2012), *Why Feeding High Fiber Kibble to Fat Cats Defies Logic*, HealthyPets.Mercola.com

Let's talk.... Blood Donation

H B Turner

Since 2007 there has been a UK blood bank for dogs. Blood collection events happen all over the country and the blood is then transported to their Loughborough laboratory to be separated into red blood cells and plasma. These are then stored and made available to veterinary surgeons upon request.

For your dog/s to qualify they must fit the following criteria:

- Fit and healthy
- Between one and 8 years old
- Weigh more than 25kg
- Have a good temperament
- Have never travelled abroad
- Vaccinated
- Not on any medication

There are collection events in: Bristol, Cheshire, Coventry, Durham, Fife, Glasgow, Leicester, Lincolnshire, Manchester, Milton Keynes, Northampton, Nottingham, Peterborough, Staffordshire, Wiltshire and many other places in between, please check the listings for the one most local to you.

The process involves a vet going through the following process with your dog prior to any donation going ahead:

- undertake a physical examination of your dog and take its health history
- carefully clip and clean a small area of your dog's neck
- microchip your dog if it not already microchipped

If all is well, your dog will go through to the donation room where a fully qualified phlebotomist will draw about 450ml of you dog's blood

Once the donation is made your dog will be brought to the refreshments area for a well earned drink and snack.

Veterinary professionals can order:

- Canine Packed Red Blood Cells (PRBC) in DEA1.1 Positive or Negative 125 or 250ml
- Canine Fresh Frozen Plasma (FFP) in 100 or 200ml
- Canine Frozen Plasma (FP) in 100 or 200ml
- Canine Cryo-Precipitate (Cryo-P)
- Canine Cryo-Supernatant (Cryo-S)
- Canine Fresh Whole Blood (FWB) in DEA1.1 Positive or Negative 225 or 450ml

Of course the qualifying criteria mean that many generous holistic pet owners who do not vaccinate &/or do not wish to microchip are unable to donate to this worth cause.

http://www.petbloodbankuk.org/

Applied Zoopharmacognosy

Karen Webb

"Animals Healing Themselves Naturally from Natures Pharmacy"

Working as a Zoopharmacognosist phrases frequently heard are; "my dog is a greedy dog or my dog is a Labrador and Labradors eat everything". Actually no they don't! Dogs are scavengers and yes if you leave a steak on the worktop it is food and they will eat it.

Food is known as a primary metabolite. A Primary Metabolite is directly involved in normal growth, development and reproduction playing a direct role in building the cell and taking part in the cellular process. They provide energy, are palatable pleasant to taste, not tasting bitter. They will include carbohydrates, proteins, enzymes and lipids. Primary metabolites are or may often be, selected when they are not immediately needed and stored as fat for later, when food is scare giving the animal an energy source.

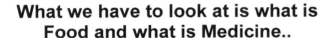

What we have to look at is what is Food and what is Medicine..

Secondary Metabolites (medicine) chemicals used by plants for purposes other than growth and reproduction. Many are highly active medicinally and are often bitter to taste. Animals will not eat secondary compounds because they are greedy, as they are not stored as fat and provide no metabolic purpose. They are only eaten for their therapeutic needs. Examples of secondary metabolites are essential oils, alkaloids, saponins, tannins etc.

Nutrients which provide vitamins and minerals are used by the body in the production of growth, energy and repair. They are not treated as staple food but as a supplement. Dogs will only select nutrients when there is a deficiency. An example of nutritional powders which contain high concentrations of vitamins and minerals are barley grass, spirulina and rosehips.

Barley grass is rich in nutrients, and is frequently selected by dogs who are anxious and hyperactive, rich in magnesium which helps to physically calm and balance the nervous system. Spirulina, an algae, is one of the richest and most easily digested forms of protein on the planet. Also rich in nutrients. It plays a vital role in the well being of many dogs.

As dog owners we're given lots of advice about giving supplements that should be added to our dogs food on a daily basis. Naturally we want to give our dogs the best to keep them healthy. We decide or are recommended how much we should give to them. We control the dosage? I would suggest that we don't actually know how much our dog needs or even if our dog wants it. Giving a dog supplements that it does not need can actually lead to problems. One of the principles in working with applied zoopharmacognosy is to never put plant compounds in the food of an animal. Why not avoid putting unnecessary supplements in food? Offer the supplements to your dog, give your dog the choice. It may be that they are only needed once or twice a week or just occasionally. Your dog knows what it needs!

Mr T. shown here always had spirulina added to his daily feed by his owner. He actually "gate crashed" a zoopharmacognosy session I had facilitated for one of the family dogs and much to the amazement of his owner helped himself to the barley grass. He knew what he needed.

It may be that they are eating grass to make themselves sick (purge) unwanted toxins from the body or they are eating a particular grass for its nutrients. Our dogs know they have a problem and need to self-medicate. Our dogs (all animals) are so clever if only we would listen to them.

A dog will be aware of what is needed to bring itself back into health and balance before symptoms manifest themselves. We as owners do not recognise our dogs have a problem until we become aware of it by seeing signs and symptoms they are displaying.

Frequently, I work with dogs who are displaying NO signs of sickness what so ever, however when offered barley grass or spirulina they will take copious

A question very often asked is why do dogs eat grass?

amounts. They may select the barley grass or spirulina to help them purge.

Purging - often happens when working with dogs. This can be for a number of reasons, to rid the body of toxins, infections or worms. It is so important that dogs have the mechanism to purge anything which is detrimental to their health. It is not unusual when working with dogs for them to select a variety of compounds such as spirulina, barley grass, fatty oils such as rice bran, sunflower, passion flower and coconut oil to help them purge.

Sometimes they will purge a huge amount of thick mucus (usually a thick slimy gunk or a watery bile, full of all sorts of debris) which has coated the debris and other harmful products, unwanted chemicals and colourants that have remained in the gut undigested, ridding the body of toxins. In which case the purged matter may be green or if also taken for nutritional value then the purged matter may not show any sign of green colouring. In some cases they will not purge at all if they needed the barley grass, spirulina or fatty oils for their nutritional value.

If toxins are in the hind gut, then purging will take the form of loose stools or diarrhoea. Purging whilst it is suggested that it usually takes place 12 to 24hrs after selecting the compounds. Frequently, it will take place either during or immediately following a zoopharmacogonosy session. Sometimes dogs may tremble before they purge, I have witnessed this in a number of dogs Dogs will often sleep once they have purged. When waking up I find they are often "like a spring chicken" as they are feeling so much better.   If purging is inhibited it may be detrimental to the dogs health.

At a recent workshop I had the privilege of facilitating two individual sessions with two super Labradors Kwazi aged 3years and Axl aged 2 years. Both had been brought along by their owners as they themselves wanted to understand self-medication together with the principles of applied zoopharmacognosy, and how to offer remedies to their dogs. They both also were interested to see if their dogs would select anything.

Both dogs were offered the same nutritional remedies during their session. Rice bran, sunflower oil,

passion flower oil, coconut oil, flax/linseed and hemp etc. When offering oils such as fixed oils, it is important that like oils are offered and not just one oil is offered. If only one oil is offered the dog may se-

lect it because it is the only oil offered and it may be selected when it is second best. Also barley grass, spirulina together with other nutritional powders.

Kwazi selected rich bran, coconut oil and barley grass. Showing no interest in the other macerated oils and dried powders. He alternated between the 3 bowls of his chosen selection. Following the session Kwazi purged.

Interestingly Axl's chosen supplements were rice bran, coconut oil and barley grass. Axl did not purge following the session.

Both were excellent demonstrations to the students that Labradors do not eat everything!! Nor do dogs always purge.

Applied Zoopharmacognosy is not intended to replace Veterinary care. If your animal is exhibiting symptoms of concern you should consult your Veterinary Surgeon.

Karen Webb Dip.IAZ

Full Practitioner Applied Zoopharmacognosy

I am available for consultations, talks, seminars and workshops

email: karen@letyouranimallead.co.uk

www.letyouranimallead.co.uk

TEL: 01740 620471
MOB: 07443043662

Reiki for Dogs
Caroline Lewis
Reiki Master Teacher

Reiki for Dogs

Caroline Lewis

Reiki is an holistic therapy providing support to all parts of the body during the healing and detoxing process. It works alongside conventional medicines.

Whilst Reiki is working, it is locating the root cause of the problem we are being faced with. Combined with working on what is presenting itself on the surface, such as skin problems, lameness, reasons behind lethargy, or behavioural difficulties as examples.

Many therapies work with 'energy' and the bodies way of handling it, particularly when put under pressure. Reiki is no different, and in Reiki these areas are known as chakras. Chakras are basically energy centres in the body. They govern our mental, emotional and physical wellbeing.

Since the last issue, I have been lucky enough to work with a number of different dogs struggling with a variety of problems. One of those was Tetley a gorgeous 12month old Lurcher. Now at such a young age, you could think not much can go wrong, but this particular dog had been in a number of placements, not including a rescue centre.

Tetley was known to have come over from Ireland and bred originally for hare coursing and hunting. At 9 weeks old he found himself at a vets in Ireland, courtesy of a very concerned person who saw him in the breeders kennels with an awful facial injury, open sores and maggots in the wounds.

Over the month Tetley was at the vets, the sores and maggots were cleared, and the wound healed. It has left him with a 4" scar which pulls at his one eye.

Unbelievably the breeder went to the vets to claim him back! The vet however had other ideas, refused to release Tetley and he went to a foster home before being brought over to the UK earlier this year to a rescue centre. In April he found himself a forever home and now the healing of the trauma can begin.

On the surface Tetley looks and behaves like any other 12 month old dog. Playful, bouncy, social, a little 'full on' but friendly. When I watched him though it became apparent that he found it very difficult to stand still, and as soon as everything around him slowed down or stopped a huge anxiety over came him and he would target another dog in the home to get a reaction and so justify his need to keep on the go.

When away from the home he reacts to other dogs, men and cars. It is

> This anxiety in turn caused his one eye to droop and become very red.

difficult to walk him anywhere stimulating because he rapidly moves from lunging, to barking and on to attacking everything. So showing that this poor dog can't cope right now. For a dog who needs to be high energy to cope with quiet surroundings, he literally has nothing left to then cope with situations outside of his control.

When I started the Reiki treatment I did ensure another dog was around because whilst he could use it as a displacement for what he was feeling (something I wasn't going to enable him to do obviously), I realised the other dog would provide comfort and reassurance whilst Tetley started to go through changes.

> He was extremely sensitive to the treatment and fascinated with what he was feeling in his body.

Initially when Tetley started to relax and his body became soft, he would race off and jump about. But equally as quickly would come back and settle right by me for another 'instalment' of the session. He loved sniffing my hands, just to see what it was he could feel I think!

In true young dog style, he suddenly flaked out and lay by my side and had a deep Reiki session. His head was uncomfortable for him initially but after a head shake he pushed himself deeper into my hands and fell fast asleep. The scar was very hot but after 5 minutes cooled right down and his eye became less drooped which was wonderful.

I found some tension in his mid thoracic area and very tight muscles around the shoulders. When this released he gave a huge stretch and truly relaxed.

During the treatment all his features softened and Tetley looked trouble free at last. The mental need to keep on the go and avoid the internal anxieties he had carried with him had disappeared, he actually enjoyed resting and sleeping for the rest of the afternoon.

After the treatment ended he chose to lie with another dog and rested for the rest of the day. This had never happened up until he received the Reiki treatment. You can see the contentment in his

whole body. But also the lovely connection with his friend which was quite a special moment to be a part of.

His owner reported that since the treatment he has stopped being on the go all the time, the muscles in his face are still relaxed so not pulling on the eye, and he is actually looking at how other dogs behave and trying to copy them. Which is far more preferable than him trying to

> "since the treatment he has stopped being on the go all the time"

tackle them head on! He also still chooses to lie with his friend, and it has been noted that he is moving a lot better now.

Tetley still has lots of fun obviously, but it is more in balance than previously and the other dogs he comes in to contact with are far more tolerant and accepting.

This was obviously only one treatment and the results have still been amazing. Whilst Tetley had had a difficult start in life, he is also still young enough to want to just let the past go. Reiki has enabled that to happen without re-visiting the traumas, which is so important to their welfare and desire to trust humans when in trouble.

Animals don't need to re-enact or relive what happened in their past. They just need to know it's safe to let go and move on.

The other bonus to his improvement is of course the other dogs in the home, who apparently are also feeling more relaxed since not being the subject of his anxieties. And of course for the owner who sees a way forward with a dog who was fast becoming reactive.

> 'only one treatment and the results have still been amazing'

When working with Reiki and animals it is not uncommon for them to make changes this quickly. I don't set out to alleviate problems straight away because I don't want them to feel shock at sudden changes. But by understanding the dog, the problems and just allowing the body to heal as it needs to, and at the rate it wants to, it does help the dog make changes quickly because we work as a team together. This is also very important because the dog needs to feel supported by someone who understands.

Each healing journey for an animal is personal to each and every one. It is a fact that is so often overlooked in trying to alleviate problems. Just because what I did with Tetley worked quickly for him, doesn't mean it would be the same for the next one. I set out to be open to all possibilities, question nothing that I see or feel, and take as long as is needed by each dog I see. That way I build an invaluable partnership with each one, and the owner too. This is essential with dogs in rescue centres, or with those that have been rehomed.

Whilst I may not have initially set out to work with dogs struggling with extreme stress, I do find myself doing this more and more. Post Traumatic Stress Disorder is a huge problem in many dogs I see, and Tetley had the potential to suffer with the same. In time a trigger for a memory buried deep inside him may emerge. When or if it does, then myself and the owner will be there for him.

A dog with Post Traumatic Stress or fears should never be forced to face them, always give choices. I saw something horrendous recently, where a trainer had gathered a number of dogs together with their owners to help the dogs face their fears of loud noises and fireworks. He set the fireworks off in the centre and every dog had a complete and utter panic attack.

> Post Traumatic Stress Disorder is a huge problem in many dogs I see

It was traumatic to watch, but to also see the dogs realisation that their owners weren't helping them was awful to see. Their trust in the one person who should always be there for them had disappeared. Of course this 'training' did not help at all, instead it will either cause some of those dogs to completely shutdown or become extremely reactive.

I have a rule I always follow. If I wouldn't want something done to me, then I will not allow it to be done to my animals. That way I know they will be ok.

Caroline Lewis

Caroline Lewis is a Reiki Master Teacher, having worked with Reiki for just over eleven years. A member of the UK Reiki Federation www.reikifed.co.uk, and The Reiki Research Centre.

Working with Dogs and Horses to encourage their improved health and wellbeing, and alleviate problems. Specialising in Post Traumatic Stress.

Providing treatments, courses, consultations and talks. Please get in touch if you wish to discuss anything in detail.

M: 07738 715195

E: caroline1706@hotmail.co.uk

Facebook: www.facebook.com/reikihorsesanddogs

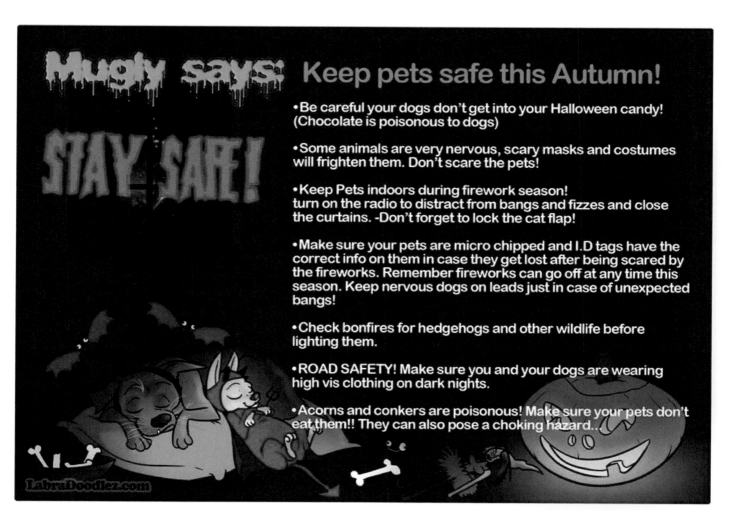

The Adventures of Mugly

By Bev Nicholson

We had lots of plans for the last couple of months but Mugly has been poorly. It is the dreaded anal glands. Mugly is 11 now and over the last couple of years he has been plagued with infections and blockages. I tried all sorts, regular expressing (by the vet!) Garlic & Fenu-greek tablets twice a day to name but a few, trying to avoid the dreaded antibiotics but he was so uncomfortable so after 2 courses sadly Mugly was no better. The decision was made to have them flushed and packed with anti-inflammatory and antibiotics. This appeared to do the trick, two weeks on he is starting to worry his back-side once again, so it is back to the internet to research something other than having them removed. Any suggestions very welcome.

Woof Factor in Cardiff was being filmed for the BBC, Fur-Baby-Crazy a 3 part series starting soon which is following the lovely Leanne Crouch from Mucky Pups in Cardiff. Mugly and I were judging the contest. We got to sit on an awesome throne.

Dog Fest in Guildford was great fun, Mia and Muppet came for the ride. We were guests of Natural Instinct who very kindly sponsor Mugly & Mia. We feed their mince as the lack of teeth in the dogs means many bones are not really an option. They are all doing very well on it. We met up with the lovely ladies from Cinque Ports Rescue including Mumble, Mia and Muppet's foster Mum who was thrilled to see them again.

Just Dogs Live saw Mugly judging the Dog's Got Talent contest, with a little of my help, the winner was a beautiful dog, adopted by a lovely young lady who has taught her all sorts of tricks. She was a Staffy Cross but a few months after her adoption she was seized under the DDA and labelled a Pit Bull Type. After a few days the court allowed her home but with a tattoo and instructions to wear a muzzle at all times in public. She was a delight to spend time with and a very worthy winner.

Mutts-Nutts had a stand in the foyer; it was quite a social event with lots of people stopping for a chat. We met some really great people and their dogs.

The highlight this quarter has to be Mugly's appearance in **John Lewis in Oxford Street**, London. He attended in his capacity of being The Ambassador of Uggly's Pet Shop toys. He went down a storm! He was a firm favourite with all the

children, a sneaked in Chihuahua and even a stalker. She waited to see him at each showing (we did 4) I chatted to lots of parents and staff, often talking about raw feeding. People were really interested; it is so satisfying to convert someone. Many of them had never heard of it, so a nice fresh audience.

We got the train home and during the journey a lady passenger complained to the steward that I was on a seat, I should add that I was on my sleeping bag and the carriage was half empty.

The steward came towards us and laughed. Turned and said to the lady, "Oh that's OK It's Mugly, he is dog royalty" It made everyone laugh, well all but one person.

Finally we also hosted our little friends 1st Gotcha Party, we had a lovely time. The dogs all dressed up to welcome our guests and dined on frozen mince filled kongs and beef jerky. Dolly has settled down beautifully in her forever home. Just love how so many people are rescuing rather than buying a pup from a breeder. It is a cause very close to our hearts. All six of my dogs are rescues, it is such a pleasure to watch them gain a little more confidence each day.

We do have our fair share of unique dogs, all of them are Chinese Cresteds, **Mugly** now 11, rescued as a pup after being handed into rescue at 3 days old. **Molly** an ex-breeding bitch, she is 4 and the most nervous, she also has dry eye sadly. **Mia** our smallest but has the biggest character, she is 3 and a half and was handed back to her breeder for being too ugly! She was passed on to rescue; we have had her for 16 months. **Lily** is 17 months and sadly has epilepsy and all sorts of allergies. We are still trying to find the best medication combination. **Madge** came next, she came from a hoarder who had 27 dogs and 20 cats, we don't know her age, her tongue hangs out as she is lacking in the tooth department. We have had her for a year; she still won't eat from a bowl and will only eat off the floor. And last but not least, **Muppet**. He is 3 and looks just like Mia. He was returned to the rescue as the previous owner had lifestyle changes.

www.Mutts-Nutts.co.uk

www.Mutts-Nutts.co.uk

THE WOLF, THE BEAR AND THE FIREMAN'S LADDER. OR, HOW I BECAME AN HOLISTIC DOG BEHAVIOURIST

Dr Isla Fishburn, BSc, MBiolSci, PhD

My story is one that is probably not too dissimilar to anyone else's story about the beginnings of how they came to work with animals, or a particular animal. Such people tend to have an early childhood gift that draws them towards their interests to the animal world. However, unlike most dog professionals that have had dogs all their lives, my story is a little different. Since early childhood (or as early as I can remember), I always wanted a dog. However, being the determined and imaginative child that I was, I didn't just want a dog but a wolf and not just any wolf mind you, but one that was small enough to fit in my pocket to travel with me on my adventures. Accompanying my real life, but small enough to fit in my pocket wolf, would be a bear (who would equally be able to be alive yet small enough to fit in my pocket!). Oh yes, and a fireman's ladder! I am not sure now of the reason why I felt the desire to have a firememan's ladder, or indeed what adventures I was planning so that my two small furry friends living in my pocket and I would ever need one. Nevertheless, a fireman's ladder was part of the plan in my young and imaginative mind. Every Christmas and Birthday came and went and, yet, no real live wild animals small enough to fit in my pocket or indeed that faithful fireman's ladder would appear. Yet, one year I did in fact get a lovely, large, far too big to fit in my pocket rabbit. He was gigantic, a lovely New Zealand white that my mother got for me from a friend at the school where she worked. The rabbit was a lovely great white ball of fluff with ruby eyes. Looking back now

where my imagination was strong for story and adventure, it was lacking for my first ever pet that I aptly named Snowie.

So, now I had no dog and certainly no wolf or bear that were alive but small enough to fit in my pocket but I did have this amazing animal that was going to join me on all my adventures. The back of my parent's house to this day reminds me of the adventures I used to have with my father and my friends. We nicknamed it the sandhills as there were lots of hills that are composed of bare earth and often looked like sand. This was the place where I would play, with friends, with my father where he would re-enact The Crystal Maze (and yes, that means he danced about like Richard O'Brien playing a pretend harmonica!), on my own...or now, with my new friend Snowie! Now, being around eight years of age, I didn't quite understand the concept of predator and prey, nor the fact that a rabbit was in fact that, and not a dog. Being kept in a hutch and only having the garden to enjoy appeared no life for my rabbit and I wanted Snowie to enjoy life as he would, had he been a dog. So, with my treats of lettuce and carrot in my pocket (that were designed for my real life wolf and bear, remember), a rabbit and only the safety of my voice to keep him from running away, off Snowie and I went to explore the sandhills and make up games of our own.

Snowie had great recall, he could hop off a few yards ahead or be sniffing and nibbling some grass, and with one call of his name he would come hopping and skipping towards me. Many a great time was spent with my rabbit and I along the paths of the sandhills. Of course, this place wasn't ours and anyone was free to roam, including dog walkers...and there were plenty of them. Snowie would simply run in to some very thick and spiky vegetation or down a hole and the dog wasn't able to get him. All the while, I still had the mindset that Snowie was going to be o.k. because he was, after all, being treated like a dog and not a rabbit. Besides, a rabbit has no real threat from a dog, right?

Looking back at it now, I can only imagine the danger Snowie must have felt when he saw a large predator bounding straight towards him that would have most certainly eaten him had it been able to. Even if this had happened I would still love dogs as much as I do.

Unfortunately, that day happened. Against all odds, Snowie wasn't actually eaten by a dog but did suddenly and sadly die one night and I was devastated – he was only one year old. Snowie was a rabbit who loved being outside and did not like going in his hutch. Not wanting to force my rabbit to do something that he was telling me he did not enjoy, I kept him outdoors for as long as I could. I think the cold, snowy, winter days were the cause of his death. On a night, I would put him in his hutch and close the door. He usually would stamp his feet in protest to be let back out. On this night, however, he went to the back of his hutch and huddled in the corner. I went to bed thinking his behaviour wasn't normal and I would see how he was in the morning. Morning came, fortunately I was also off school with a bad cold, and it looked like Snowie had developed a cold too. But, his cold was different to mine. He was quiet, still and did not greet me when I went to his hutch. I knew something was up. I brought him in to the house immediately and wrapped him in a blanket and held him tight near to the heater. After about 30 minutes he gave one almighty scream (which I can still hear to this day) and died in my arms. My dear animal friend who I spent so much time with had gone. It took me a while to get over.

Just from that one experience I was plagued with terrors that I was cursed. That any other animal I would get would only live for a year and then all that love, sharing and bond would be ripped away from me. I was eight years old and already giving myself a hard time about an event that was just natural. I would like to say the reason for my harsh outlook and my "curse" was because I had a difficult childhood or something similar where I was experienced with let down and hardship. This was on the contrary; my parents were always so supportive, loving and affectionate. It makes me giggle looking back at how hard I was on myself and believing I was cursed. Yet, it was something that haunted me for many years and whilst I urged to have a dog I got my "fix" from walking the dogs of my friend's and family.

The desire to have my own dog became too much. Having access to scientific papers on animal behaviour whilst at university were just the teasers I needed to make the decision to get a dog and that is where it all started. I love dogs, I always have, and throughout my childhood I knew I wanted to work with wildlife. This quickly developed in to wanting to specifically work with megafauna and predators. Then, as I matured I wanted to work in Canid conservation.

Spending time working with wolves and teaching people about conservation, I began to meet people who had dogs and who truly loved them. Yet, frequent statements such as "I love taking my dog to the pub," or "I love taking my dog on holiday" made me begin to question if what they were doing really was what their dog also loved. It made me think of Snowie and how he hated going in his hutch at night yet I didn't understand or consider the reasons why, or that I would take him on a walk without thinking about his needs. As I began to do more and more observation work and reading about canine behaviour, the more and more I began to realise that we may think our dogs share the same passion as us, but if we really do love our dogs then shouldn't we be as sure as we possibly can that our dogs are happy in what we do, where we take them and how we interact with them? How do we know that our dogs are happy and what can we do to help them if they are not? All this is about safety.

Whilst studying for my PhD I began to read literature on how wild animals adopt an holistic approach to safeguard themselves and their survival. Why should a dog (or any domestic animal) be any different? Ultimately, every animal's priority is their survival. An animal that feels safe (or whose wellbeing is not compromised) is going to show a very different behaviour, feeling, outlook and energy than an animal that does not feel safe. What may be one dog's pleasure may be another dog's fear and it is recognising that dog's have individual preferences, tolerances, coping mechanisms and survival sensitivities that can be explained by looking at the different causes of behaviour.

Today, as a Zoologist I consider each animal first and foremost as a living biological organism that responds differently to its world than what we do. Dogs are no different. And, as a zoologist, my passion in animal behaviour is to consider the individual differences of a species, the causes of these differences and how a dog as a social group animal prioritises its survival. It is these individual differences that I consider when working with dogs. Dogs do have emotions; it is these emotions that are the foundations of any mammal's

survival.

Dogs are sentient beings that are constantly observing, listening, learning and, most importantly, feeling. I use knowledge of canine social behaviour and ecology to help improve or understand dog behaviour and wellbeing. As such I consider the emotional, mental and physical wellbeing of a dog and work with each dog as an individual. To complement the work that I do, I also use natural healing and/or Applied Zoopharmacognosy to support the animal and to help him/her improve how they are feeling.

In addition, as a dog's human guardian and with dogs being social animals, I also believe it is important that humans who co-exist with dogs also take a great interest in their own wellbeing. Sometimes, a dog can show a behavioural response because of their exposure to human role models; we all have times in our lives where we are stressed, anxious, angry or over-worked. I believe that we inadvertently impose our own emotional, physical and spiritual strains, stresses or conflicts on to our dog. If we are stressed, so is our dog and they can change their behavioural response simply as a result of who and how we are. My focus is about the overall wellbeing of a dog and to create an environment that is calm, peaceful and safe. Knowing that how a person is feeling can affect a dog's wellbeing, I also offer human guardian healing to help improve the wellbeing of those that a dog lives with, so that both human and dog can live in harmony and trust.

I do not believe that you can ever stop learning (and if you think you can then you had best move on to a new subject of interest) I therefore expect my knowledge and understanding of dogs to evolve; when I was eight years old I thought I could have two perfectly fully functioning wild animals of a miniature size living in my pocket. Of course, I quickly realised the impossibility of such a con-

Volume 2 Issue 3 September 2015

cept. In a similar light, to help others as well as dogs themselves you have to work with the current knowledge and research that is present as long as you accept that in order to truly understand your subject of interest one must continually find the passion, enthusiasm and desire to learn more. My work is therefore based on the knowledge of my current understanding, observations and research that I would like to share with you and should evolve as we all learn more about canines.

NURTURE THEM NATURALLY

We specialise in creating a range of homeopathic, herbal and natural products to improve the health and lifestyle of your pet.

With everything from natural alternatives to flea powders, Worming control and supplements to a fabulous chemical free bathing range.

Everything we produce is 100% chemical free

NURTURETHEMNATURALLY.CO.UK

Isla is on the panel of experts for the Dog Welfare Alliance and is a member of Association of IN-TODogs (Intuitive Natural Training for Owners and Dogs). She is one of only a few behaviourists that are affiliated with the International School of Canine Practitioners (ISCP) and is part of their affiliation programme. She is a member of the International Society of Athrozoology(ISAZ). Adopting an holistic approach to helping your dog, Isla is passionate about hepling improve your dog's emotional, mental and physical wellbeing and considers both complementary medicine that can be used in conjunction with conventional veterinary procedures. As such, Isla is working towards practitioner status in zoopharmacognosy, Bach Flower Remedies as well as energy healing.

www.kachinacaninecommunication.co.uk

Kachina Canine Communication

Communication

There are several types of communication when it comes to animals.

- How we understand them
- How they understand us
- How they understand each other

I can guarantee that the first two on this list have been misinterpreted at one time or another by owner and pet in your household.

Another method is by finding an 'Animal Communicator' or 'Animal Medium' if you will, who can communicate psychically with your pet. Many may scoff, however when a complete stranger supplies you with information only you, your family and your pet might know it is difficult to deny that there are those out there with true ability.

http://www.animalinterpreters.co.uk/

Facebook/animalinterpreters

MY DOG HAS PARATHYROIDISM

By Ruth Lomax

Human, Equine and Animal Therapist – Bowen Technique, Scenar Cosmodic Therapy, Bio-Resonance, EFT, Reiki.

My gorgeous little dog Jenny, a Jack x Yorkie, stopped eating a year last February. She has always been a picky eater, refusing commercial dog food at the first taste of something better and I knew I had probably taught her to be picky so when she started refusing everything offered yet showed no other signs of illness or behaviour changes I went through all the logical explanations and decided for once I was not giving in to her and that when she was really hungry she would eat something. She was chewing her feet and scratching so I treated her for fleas.

This went on for 7 whole days before my worries couldn't contain themselves any longer, I knew there was something really wrong and no dog would voluntarily starve herself for so long. She had also wet the bed in the night a couple of times which was very unlike her. I took her to my local vet who realised she was very dehydrated yet she had been drinking plenty and weeing what I realised later was rather a lot. With the lack of food she was quite weak. She was kept in for a couple of days on a drip to rehydrate her. They managed to tempt her to eat something bland then she came home and I took over the feeding. She began to eat more normally.

Over the next 3 weeks her appetite went up and down and she was sick on a few occasions, she was still drinking and weeing quite a lot (Polydipsia and Polyuria) but didn't seem to be getting particularly dehydrated. Other symptoms began to show including muscle twitches in her front legs, unusually tight neck and shoulders (so I treated her with Bowen Technique) , more accidents during the night and one or two during the day. She clearly had no clue she was urinating at the time. She was soaked through in the morning…as was my bed!

At the same time, her energy levels dropped and she was tired at the end of walks, she was becoming very anxious and irritable, particularly with other dogs and with the slightest of noises. Every little thing seemed to upset her and set her off into shakes. She was becoming very clingy and she was bringing her food back more often. She began whimpering in her sleep. Her twitches rapidly developed into muscle spasms which were so strong and sudden, on a few occasions she literally seemed to flip from one side of my bed to the other or off the bed entirely. I actually thought at first she had been bitten by a flea!

All of these symptoms had developed very quickly. And I was completely baffled as to what was causing them so I took her back to my local vet and she told me she thought it could be a Parathyroid issue. We did blood tests for Calcium (Ca) and Parathyroid Hormone (PHT) levels, a full blood analysis to establish what the cause was and Urinalysis to check for infection and kidney involvement.

The results were shocking. Her ionised calcium count was 0.25 (normal range is 1.25 – 1.65) which meant that she had very little calcium in her blood stream. Her PHT levels were also very low. Her Specific Gravity was very weak (very watery urine). She was suffering from Hypocalcemia as a result of Hypoparathyroidism. Something had gone badly wrong with her Parathyroid glands and it didn't seem to be producing the Parathyroid Hormone which regulates calcium levels in the body.

We immediately put her on 2 tabs of Calcium Lactate 2x a day. 3 weeks later we tested but there was little change so Vit D3 capsules (NB only Rocaltrol can be given to dogs as a Vit D supplement as other types or toxic to them) was added daily to help absorption. Her calcium levels started to creep back up and some of the symptoms began to subside. Her appetite improved, her muscle twitching stopped, her bed wetting was less but she was still very anxious and clingy.

Unfortunately she was then a victim of a nasty unprovoked dog attack which she did not see coming. She went into shock and terror so I gave her Aconite homeopathic and some Bowen Technique but that night she had a total body seizure (in the Hypocalcemic picture) lasting 15 seconds or more. It was extremely frightening to watch. I took her to the emergency vet for a thorough check up before sleeping on the floor with her.

A few weeks later her calcium levels hit normal but then she started to refuse food again, wet the bed a lot, was looking rather stiff as though she had pulled a muscle, was still very anxious and again was increasingly aggressive with other dogs. She seemed depressed and I began to notice that she wasn't following her toys as well when I threw them.

Further blood tests revealed she had gone way over the normal calcium range and was extremely *HYPER*CALCEMIC! Her calcium supplements were dropped to 1 ½ tabs 2x daily but it didn't seem to make much difference. I raised my concerns re the eyes (which were going worse) and the fact that her kidney energy was unbalanced but the vet dismissed any connection with the calcium levels. My own internet research had revealed the connection so I made the executive decision to reduce her tabs to just 1 twice a day and took her to see my holistic vet, Sue Armstrong in Wetherby. She told me Jenny could have died if I hadn't reduced the dose!

We immediately set about retesting everything including testing the Thyroid glands in case they were affected too. Thankfully they were not. Urine tests were included and some bloods were sent to Jean Dodd in America for careful analysis. Poor little Jenny was a pin cushion with all the blood tests but she has been an absolute star about it. Her neck was thoroughly examined and scanned for lumps. There were none.

Unfortunately it has taken a lot to reduce her calcium levels again, many weeks have gone by and we have further reduced the supplementation bit by bit. You cannot rush this as the body cannot cope with big calcium level swings. To add to the problem she began to refuse to go for a walk 3 months ago. She would refuse to go round the corner of my house for our normal evening walk, she would refuse to get out of the car at an increasing number of places. Some places clearly were linked to some bad incidents with dogs in the past including a very nasty couple of attacks. Some were linked to noises she heard that frightened her but some were absolutely baffling and frustrating. It began to affect our whole lives.

Jenny has had Rocaltrol daily throughout. Jenny knew her calcium was still high and often tried to refuse a tablet but as we needed to know categorically through blood tests, I had to keep giving her whatever amount we were trying. Finally, after months of careful monitoring we think she may be there. She is currently on a 2 day system - 1 Rocaltrol once every 2 days and on one day she has 2x ¼ tablet and on the next day she has just 1x ¼ . We are waiting for the last results as I type. Her behavioural issues have shown a marked return to normal, our walks are long and enjoyable again and her overall confidence is returning.

BUT she is licking her forelegs a lot again and her appetite is going off!!!!!!!!!!!!!!

Have we gone a step too far????

Volume 2 Issue 3 September 201!

So......WHAT IS PARATHYROIDISM?

Parathyroid Glands are small endocrine glands located next to the Thyroid Glands, at the front of the neck. They have nothing to do with Thyroids in function. They have their own very important function – producing Parathyroid Hormone or PTH.

PTH precisely regulates the amount of Calcium (Ca) and Phosphorous (Ph) in the blood stream to be taken to tissues which need them. An *increase* in PTH increases the blood calcium and decreases the amount of Phosphorous. A *decrease* in PHT production reduces the amount of calcium in the blood.

If the Parathyroid Glands produce insufficient PTH (Hypoparathyroidism) there will be insufficient calcium in the bloodstream (Hypocalcaemia). If calcium isn't present in the diet, it will be taken from the bones and Osteomalacia or brittle bones may occur. On the other hand if the Parathyroid glands are producing too much PTH (Hyperparathyroidism) there will be too much calcium in the bloodstream. Excess calcium is excreted by the kidneys but if the excess amount is continually high, kidney and bladder stones may form (Hypercalcaemia).

WHY DOES IT HAPPEN?

Hypoparathyroidism occurs rarely but for a variety of reasons

If the Parathyroid glands themselves become damaged through injury, parathyroid surgery, or indirectly during Thyroid surgery. (*NB We think Jenny's were damaged when I had to pull her up by her collar and lead to get her out of a life threatening situation with 2 Akitas and a German Shepherd which Jenny in her wisdom had decided to take on!*)

Starvation (not just 7 days).

Congenital abnormality where the glands have not formed properly or maybe absent.

Tumour / Cancer

Genetic predisposition - certain breeds of dog such as St Bernard, German Shepherd, Poodles, Terriers and Cross breeds had a higher incidence though overall Parathyroid issues are considered rare.

Infection

Systemic and Auto- immune disorders (Secondary Hypoparathyridism).

Magnesium deficiency in rare cases.

In all cases, the resulting symptoms are due to a lowering of Calcium in the blood stream – Hypocalcemia.

Calcium is a mineral obtained from food - meat bones, fish bones (tinned), milk, cheese, yoghurt, green leafy veg (not spinach), soya beans, tofu, bread and fortified flour products, hard water, and fillers in some medications and supplements as calcium carbonate or chalk .

Calcium is needed for many very important and sensitive functions –

Form and strengthen bones and teeth (99% of Ca in the body)

Act as part of the chemical message transmission in nerve conduction controlling contraction and relaxation of all skeletal muscle creating movement and posture,

Help contraction of the cardiac muscle of the heart

Normal functioning of smooth muscle responsible for ongoing involuntary contractions in the intestines, stomach, uterus, bladder, and other tube like structures.

Contributes to normal brain function

Stabilises Blood Pressure

Blood clotting

Helps Insulin open cells to glucose

Assists the sperm movement into the egg to fertilise it.

Phosphorous is a mineral found in most foods and is needed for the formation of bones and teeth plus many metabolic functions. When Hypocalcaemia occurs, so does the corresponding Hyperphosphatemia (increase in blood phosphorous).

So you see… if the amount of blood calcium is not regulated properly, most conscious and unconscious muscle contractions will be affected, the heart may be affected, the nervous system and brain are affected having massive knock on effects throughout the body and many other sensitive functions in cells and tissues can be affected.

A dog will feel very ill and peculiar indeed.

Hypocalcemia occurs as a direct result of *Hypo*parathyroidism, insufficient or mal absorption of dietary calcium, insufficient dietary Vitamin D3 (needed to absorb Calcium into the bloodstream), Kidney failure.

Symptoms include Muscle twitching, Spasms, Polydipsia (drinks a lot), Polyuria (urinates a lot), Depressed appetite, Anorexia (self starvation), Depression, Stiff gait, Cramping, Cataracts, Fearfulness, Clinginess, Loss of confidence generally, Lethargy, Tetany (rigid muscles) and eventually Death.

Secondary symptoms may develop including reduced kidney function, loss of sight, heart palpitations, more developed behavioural changes.

Hypercalcemia can be a direct result of *Hyper*parathyroidism, too much Ca supplementation, tumours, under functioning Adrenal Glands, Vit D poisoning from rat poison, Vit D over supplementation, Aluminium toxicity.

Symptoms include Polydipsia, Polyuria, Anorexia, Vomiting, Poor gastric function, Constipation, Fatigue, Depression, Bladder and Kidney stones, Cataracts, Hypertension, Coma and eventually Death.

The similarities between the two ends of the spectrum can be confusing when a dog is swinging between Hypo and Hypercalcemia. This is why blood tests are so vital.

<u>HOW DO YOU TREAT IT?</u>

Even if the glands need removing due to a tumour, treatment for Hypocalcemia or Hypercalcemia is always to balance the Calcium and Phosphorous within the body. Calcium Lactate and Vitamin D3 (essential for absorption of Calcium) supplements must be given daily, in the correct quantities for balance. The only way to establish the correct balance and ensure its correct maintenance level is regular blood tests looking at both ordinary calcium levels and ionised calcium (main cellular functioning type of calcium) levels and PHT levels.

Complementary treatments MAY help encourage the Parathyroid glands to heal if damaged and possibly produce a better natural level of PHT but it would be dangerous to assume so. I do think that some of the therapy sessions I have given Jenny have helped to reduce the amount of supplementation needed but she will always need monitoring and will always need some supplementation.

To contact Ruth for Human, Equine or Animal Treatments –

Tel – Mob 0794 767 2815 Home 01422 839789

Email – <u>ruth.lomax@googlemail.com</u>

Association for Non-Veterinary Natural Animal Health Practitioners

ANNAHP AWARDS

The winners in the first annual ANNAHP awards as voted by you the readers are:-

- ### Best Holistic Therapy Article

Julie Moss

Best Behaviour Animal Therapy

Introducing Tellington Touch

Healthful Dog 1[2]:82-83

- ### Best Food Article

H B Turner

Healthful

Dental Chews

Healthful Dog 2[1]:48-49

- ### Best Health Article

Caroline Hearn

Holistic Hounds

Worming Dogs & the Alternatives

Healthful Dog 2[2]:104-105

- ## Most Interesting Article

Julie Arnold

Naturally Healthy Dogs

Our Own Journey to a Raw Diet

Healthful Dog 2[2]:129

- ## Most Helpful Article

Catherine O'Driscoll

Canine Health Concern

VacciCheck—The Way Forward

Healthful Dog 1[1]:35

Congratulations to our award winning contributors and many thanks to you the readers for voting.

www.annahp.co.uk

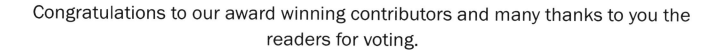

The Association of Non-Veterinary Natural Animal Health Practitioners (ANNAHP)

ANNAHP is an association created for respected and qualified natural animal health practitioners, for clients and veterinary surgeons to have a trustworthy body to refer to.

www.annahp.co.uk

Debono Moves
From Hip Dysplasia to Agility

Mary Debono, GCFP

Emma was even more energetic than your typical Border Collie pup. And if you've spent any time around Border Collies, you know that is saying a lot!

Strikingly marked, the active black and white puppy enlivened Akiko and Michael's household from the minute they brought her home. Given the dog's naturally high drive, Akiko had hopes of entering Emma in canine agility competitions when she matured. But that dream appeared to be dashed when the seven month old puppy was diagnosed with severe hip dysplasia. The radiographs looked pretty grim, with the left hip being particularly loose. Both hips had a positive Ortolani sign, which indicates hip joint laxity and is part of the diagnostic procedure for canine hip dysplasia.

More than one veterinarian felt that the only way to give the young dog a chance at a pain-free life was by doing triple pelvic osteotomy (TPO) surgery on the left hip. But Akiko had concerns about her dog undergoing surgery. For one thing, she didn't think that her exuberant young dog could handle the long period of post-surgical confinement. Another factor was that Akiko had been down this road before. Her beloved Akita, a gentle soul named Winnie, had undergone hip dysplasia surgery as a youngster. And while the surgery repaired her hips, the changes it created in her structure seemed to adversely affect her knees and back, leaving Winnie with difficulties in her hind legs throughout her long life. Understandably, Akiko was reluctant to risk this happening to her young Border Collie, Emma.

Debono Moves is part of a team approach to managing hip dysplasia

Would changing the way the young dog moved stimulate healthier hip joints?

Keeping her dog's well-being uppermost in her mind, Akiko opted to support Emma using conservative management and alternative therapies. A diligent researcher, petite, raven-haired Akiko employed a team approach to help her Border Collie. Her veterinarian incorporated chiropractic, laser acupuncture[1], and other holistic methods. Akiko had always provided her dog with a professionally-balanced, home-prepared diet designed for a growing puppy. That diet was now modified to meet adult nutrient levels to slow the young Border Collie's growth. Emma's diet was also supplemented with herbs and nutraceuticals to support joint and bone health. In addition, Akiko asked me to give private *Debono Moves* sessions to Emma to help mitigate the effects of her hip dysplasia.

Although I understood that hip dysplasia is often genetically pre-destined, I wanted to improve the young dog's odds of staying sound and active. I began to wonder if changing how Emma moved would stimulate her body to develop healthier hip joints. After all, *form follow function*. If I could help improve her *function* (ability to walk, run, etc.), would her *form* (structure) improve as well? Could the pup's hip joints, which

---

1 Laser acupuncture uses cold lasers, rather than needles, to treat acupuncture points.

were still growing, develop a better fit between the "ball" and "socket"?

A tall order, for sure. But I knew that at the very least, *Debono Moves* could help the young dog move more comfortably *despite* hip dysplasia. At the most, it might stimulate the development of healthier hip joints.

One strategy I used with Emma was to *chunk down* the function of walking into small pieces. In other words, I thought about the individual movements of a dog's body that, when strung together, result in walking. By working with each piece of this walking "puzzle", Emma wouldn't feel the need to protect her hips, and would be more likely to learn healthier ways to move.

For example, when a dog walks, she has to push against the ground with her paws. That seems simple enough. But exactly *how* she does this can determine the comfort and efficiency of her gait. Does she press more with the inside of her foot? The outside? Are her toes stiff or yielding? Does one paw press harder than the others? These are the types of distinctions I look for when I watch a dog move, since the way a dog uses her paws affects her knees, hips, spine, shoulders and neck. So, with Emma lying on her side, I gently wiggled and pushed through her toes and paw pads.

> I wanted to give Emma the experience of moving as if she didn't have hip dysplasia

The novelty of these gentle paw movements reminded the Border Collie that she didn't have to be stuck in her habitual way of using her feet. She could, instead, choose more efficient options. After all, the brain seeks efficiency. It just sometimes needs to be reminded that options exist. When I delicately moved her feet, I was simply suggesting new choices. Whether or not her brain adopted those new movement possibilities would be up to Emma. But this I knew: if the dog changed the way she used her paws, she would change the way movement traveled up her legs and through her hip joints. Her nervous system would register this change in locomotion[2].

> It was important to relieve the strain throughout the dog's body

With Emma still on her side, I brought in other components of walking, including bending and straightening her leg joints, flexing and extending her spine, and moving her ribcage, shoulder blades, neck, head and tail. Then I began to link these movements together, so that Emma's nervous system could recognize the role they played in her walking. In addition, I thought about how the Border Collie would move if she didn't have hip dysplasia. How would her leg joints respond to weight and movement? How differently would she move her spine? With Emma both lying down and standing up, I gently pressed through different parts of her skeleton to stimulate, as best I could, how she might move without the encumbrance of hip dysplasia. I hoped that this rudimentary "blueprint" would awaken something in her nervous system and initiate improvements in her body awareness and functioning[3].

As always, I kept *all* of Emma in mind as I worked with her. Dogs with hip dysplasia (or any hind limb soreness), commonly stress their shoulder, back and pelvic muscles to compensate for the discomfort or weakness in their hind legs. I used *Debono Moves* to help relieve the strain in those overworked areas, and helped Emma be more comfortable and balanced overall.

2 Joint movements activate receptors that relay information to the nervous system regarding limb movement, joint angle and muscle tension. This information is used to coordinate movement.

3 If a dog has a hip problem, it is likely that the dog has learned to compensate for the painful hip by tensing muscles around the hip joints and spine, among other places. Even in a healed injury, the body may continue to contract these muscles out of habit. By gently pressing through the pelvis, I initiate movement into the body while bypassing the legs entirely. This means that the dog has no reason to tighten the muscles that would protect against potentially painful hips, since the hips are not involved. Thus the dog has the sensory experience of movement, but free of its usual interference. Such pleasurable experiences are sometimes enough for a dog's nervous system to recognize that its habitual contractions are no longer serving a useful purpose, and can release them. This strategy can be applied to many situations, not just hip difficulties.

Volume 2 Issue 3 September 201

X-rays reveal a surprising change in the Border Collie's hips

Just in case you are picturing me working with a relaxed, somnolent dog, let me share my reality! Emma, despite the diagnosis of hip dysplasia, continued to be very energetic. That meant that I had to be flexible in our sessions, as the vibrant young dog didn't always want to lie still. But dogs don't have to lie still for *Debono Moves* to be effective. When I work with very antsy dogs, their humans often call me the day after the session. With surprise in their voice, they tell me how much better their dog is moving. They confess to having thought that we hadn't accomplished much since their dog was distracted during the session. I remind them that although we could probably progress faster with a relaxed dog, even a distracted dog will typically benefit from *Debono Moves*.

The Border Collie became calmer and more relaxed as time went on, due largely to Akiko's patience in teaching Emma that lying still and being handled would earn her yummy treats. Akiko also supported her dog's progress by practicing specific *Debono Moves* that I taught her in between my sessions with Emma. Soon the young Border Collie realized how nice it felt to lie still and enjoy hands-on attention! Emma still got excitable when I visited her home, but we accomplished more and more at each session.

As the months went by, the young dog became stronger and more balanced in her movement and development. Emma's hips were x-rayed again, almost a year after the diagnosis of hip dysplasia.

Take a look at the radiographs to see what a difference a year makes! Pay special attention to how Emma's left hip joint (which is on the right side of each photo) fits into its' hip socket. The disparity between the two x-rays in quite dramatic. In the first one, taken in October 2010, the left hip is obviously loose, and there are signs of arthritic changes.

The second radiograph, taken in September 2011, shows the head of each femur now fitting nicely into its hip socket, and the veterinarian said there is no longer evidence of arthritis. This was, of course, exciting and fantastic news!

The third photo is Emma's radiograph from September 2012. It again shows a dog with healthy hips. And as icing on the cake, the Orthopedic Foundation for Animals (OFA) gave two year-old Emma's hips a rating of "Good". This was very surprising results for a dog whose "only option" had been surgery!

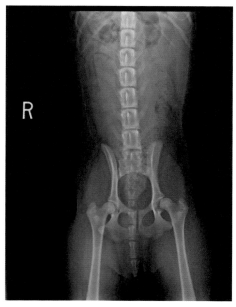

X-ray October 2010

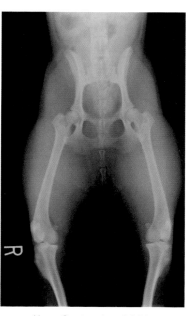

X-ray September 2011

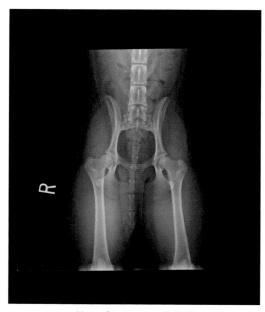

X-ray September 2012

With her dog's soundness more secure, Akiko and Emma happily began canine agility training, an activity that seemed out of reach when the young dog was first diagnosed.

Since a holistic veterinarian and a canine nutritionist also contributed to Emma's care, we have no way of knowing what exact role Debono Moves played in the Border Collie's recovery from hip dysplasia. What we do know is that a veterinary orthopedist said that Emma's his would never improve. And yet Emma's x-rays—and more importantly, her ability to run and play—tell a very different story. My feeling is that all of the modalities, including *Debono Moves*, helped support this young dog's development of healthy hip joints and contributed to her wonderful and surprising recovery.

Emma went from hip dysplasia to healthy hips!

But at the end of the day, I give the greatest credit to Akiko and her husband, Michael. Their steadfast dedication to their vibrant dog is inspiring. Akiko's patient commitment to do her *Debono Moves* homework with her exuberant Border Collie helped improve her dog's body awareness and functioning, taught her how to be calm and relaxed, and deepened their strong bond.

Mary Debono is the author of the Amazon best seller, Grow Young with Your Dog. A Certified Feldenkrais® Practitioner, Mary teaches people how to create healthy, active lives with their animal companions, while minimizing the effects of injury and aging. She lives in Southern California with her husband, horse, dog and cat.

www.DebonoMoves.com

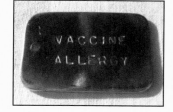

Golden Oldies

Caring for the Elderly Dog

Caroline Hearn

As our beloved dogs age their requirements change, so here are a few tips to make a positive difference to the health and mobility of your senior dog.

Keep their weight in check. Being overweight will overload their joints and cause excessive strain to their heart and lungs, and potentially knock years off their life. Seek advice about dietary needs of the senior, particularly if dealing with diabetes or kidney problems. Talk to a holistic vet or therapist about changing to a more natural diet and away from processed foods.

There are many supplements for aging dogs which can help with mobility and other health issues brought on by old age. Glucosamine and Chondroitin have been popular for some time, but also try some of the herbal supplements for general health and well being. Adding Omega oils is a great idea for joint health, skin and coat condition and can reduce inflammation. Many people have seen improvement in their own and their dogs' mobility after including turmeric paste into their diets. Natural chews such as trachea and chicken feet contain high levels of glucosamine which your dog will find easier to utilise as it is from a naturally occurring source.

Use a car ramp, it is so much kinder to your dogs joints, particularly to their shoulders, than jumping in and especially out of the car. There are many on the market, but make sure you get one which has non slip footing and that it is user friend for you to handle. Take time to get them with used to

going up and down, and use treats if necessary; you may have to support them with your arms, or a rolled up towel around their chest and bottom to steady a frail or blind dog, to make them feel secure. Try to discourage elderly dogs going up and down stairs as this can also cause strain on their joints plus the added risk of falling.

Ensure your dog has a soft bed, which offers protection and support for their joints. Some dogs love to stretch right out and others curl in a ball, so bear this in mind when choosing a bed. If you have hard plastic beds make sure they are big enough so the dog isn't forced into an uncomfortable shape and has a soft base of bedding. A slightly raised bed may also help with getting up and down.

You may well find that your dog is far more comfortable eating and drinking from raised bowls, which takes the strain off their neck, back and shoulders. There are many on the market, but I have found the cheap plastic ones which stack together do the trick and you can adjust the number of bowls until it is just the right height for them. Then you can just add a stainless steel bowl into the top which are easier to keep really clean.

Exercise requirements will start to change and if he over exerts himself it will show in the days that follow. If the dog loves to run free, always make sure they are warmed up on the lead for ten minutes or so before letting off. Try to cut right down or stop altogether sudden bursts of movement, such as ball throwing and tug of war etc. as this can cause a lot of strain to their body and is a common cause of lameness.

If your dogs eyesight and hearing is failing then personally I think they are safer on a lead. If you use a harness, then make sure it is roomy enough so you don't have t bend arthritic joints to get it on. If you have very elderly or frail dogs, then all they need is a gentle stroll, or stretch their legs in the garden. It is so upsetting seeing people dragging their old dogs behind the, it stresses them and does nothing for their wellbeing.

Regular massage is really helpful to keep him mobile and will also pick up on any injury, muscle wastage or tightness. Ask your therapist for some homework you can do between treatments. Many people have had success with magnet therapy in the form of collars or inserted into bedding, gradually introduce these if you choose to use them. A heat pad can be useful in cold weather, as can a comfortable fleece coat, especially if your struggle to keep weight on the dog.

I have found acupuncture and homeopathy to be excellent in treating mobility problems.

Watch out for unexplained weight loss, excessive drinking, lumps or swellings, changes in behaviour, discomfort while eating, or difficulty going to the toilet, they should always be investigated by your vet as soon as possible.

Enjoy your treasured senior companion.

Caroline is a sports & remedial massage therapist, treating human, equine and canine clients. Dogs are her first love and she has three Labradors.

www.holistic-hounds.co.uk

caroline@holistic-hounds.co.uk

Pet Loss Oasis—"How Did My Animal Die?"
When Intuitive Animal Communication can clarify – and why it can sometimes confuse.
By Sue Reid with Elaine Downs, Interspecies Communicators and Energy

For me, naturally, Interspecies Communication (also known as Intuitive Animal Communication) is the way to understand our animals better, get to the heart of what's troubling or hurting them, and to create a relationship with them that is so close and trusting that it can feel almost magical. It's an ancient skill that we all have but which most of us allow to lie dormant apart from odd flashes of inspiration which we may dismiss as coincidence. But never is this skill more needed than around the time of their final journey, when every word and every moment is so precious, and all we want is to get it right for them.

When a beloved animal family member dies, there is almost always heartbreak, grief and pain. Hard enough when the death is expected. But when an apparently young and healthy animal is found dead, with no indication of how or why, this brings with it so many questions that healing and closure can feel impossible.

This is what happened to a lady who contacted one of our Facebook pages recently for help. Her beautiful soulmate cat had been found dead, with no clue as to the reason. She was devastated, and desperate to know what had happened.

Several people immediately came for-ward to help, and offered to communicate with her cat in spirit at no charge, which she gratefully accepted. But soon after, she contacted me with a question, the nub of which was:-

"I have had many lovely people contact me and communicate with my cat, and I am truly grateful. So much of what they said was similar, and I found it very comforting. But some of the information was conflicting about how she died. I know that everyone is doing their very best. Can you help me understand when the information I receive is true, and when it is not?"

This is a very fair question. Because Intuitive Animal Communication, like mediumship, uses our subtle senses rather than our knowledge or brain power, it can sometimes require interpretation; and there are times when it can appear contradictory or even just plain wrong. Very few Intuitive Animal Communicators, including myself, would say that they have always had every single detail of every communication correct.

But it's vital that those who seek the help of an interspecies communicator, understand something of how this type of communication works, and why the information received may not always fit into a neat package of questions and answers in exactly the same way as a verbal conversation might; why conflicting information or inaccuracies can sometimes occur; and how to create the best chance of getting what they feel they need from an animal communication session.

This is important both for their own peace of mind; maybe for their own personal growth if that's their interest; and for the recognition of Intuitive Animal Communication itself as a very real, universal skill which has the power to change our relationships with other species, as well as our perception of death and dying, for ever.

So after some deliberation, this was my answer:-

"First, how lovely that so many people have come forward to help you, and without charge.

The only downside of having a number of people involved is that because animal communication works by connecting the frequency range of your animal to that of the communicator, you may get some variation in the message as each one of us will have access to slightly different frequencies.

Also, because of individual strengths, and varying development level, some communicators work best with words, some with pictures, some with feelings, so there will be differences in depth, in interpretation and in the way the messages come across.

At Animal Matters, Elaine and I find that the best way to ensure we have a valid connection is to work either face to face or with a photograph, and offer some validation in terms of personality description, or some other information so that our client can either say Yes, you have my animal with you, or No, I don't think that connection is strong enough. On the basis of that introductory time, the client can choose to continue with the communication or not.

But everyone works differently. And sometimes you can be drawn to particular people for reasons you don't fully understand, but which may come clear later.

If you feel unsure whether one of the communicators had a good connection with your cat, you could ask that person if they were willing/able to give you more evidence that would help you decide whether the message was valid. There can be a lot to be said for getting really quiet within yourself, and sitting with your heart feeling. Not easy when you're grieving, I know, and I sympathise. But it's possible that this current confusion is a part of your own journey with your cat, and with animal communication. Keep sending her love, and stay open to receiving any message she may want to send you. And follow your heart about what to do next and when to do it.

So sorry that this probably isn't the simple straightforward answer you would have wished for (or that I would have been looking for if I were in your position). Of course you can simply try another communicator if that feels right. But no one can guarantee whether that would clarify or add to your confusion. Just stay strong in your love for your precious cat, and know that her love will be always there for you. And then let the right action present itself.

With love,
Sue xxxx"

Her answer was full of love and gratitude to everyone who had helped her, and a commitment to honour her relationship with her cat by further developing her own intuitive animal communica-

tion skills so she could also help others. The full truth about her beloved cat's death may never be known for sure. But what is known is that love transcends death; and that when people come together in good intent to help and support each other through pain and suffering, then what is shared is love, and the world is a better place for that.

So that beautiful little cat, by her manner of death, opened up doors of possibilities for development that might have remained for ever closed if this had not happened as it did. No-one would have wished it so. But there it is. And discovering purpose in the pain, can offer a way towards healing, in its own time and space.

How to maximise connection and minimise confusion

The more we can develop our own intuitive connection with our animals, the deeper our knowledge and understanding of each other, and the less we need others to help us make that connection. But to reach this stage we have to be prepared to put their needs before our own, and to hear the unhearable, if that is what their truth is. It can be a big ask, especially if we're already overwhelmed with grief and trauma around their leaving.

What I do is to have just one or two specific people who I approach in these circumstances, who I already know and trust, and who have given me deep messages from my animals that I know to be accurate. That way, I'm as confident as I can be that everyone has been heard and honoured, so the way forward can be clear. I don't always need them, but it's good to know they're there if I do.

So you can do two things right now, to minimise the stress and confusion if/

when an emergency should arise:-

1. Recognise and practice your own intuitive communication skills. Work with a sympathetic friend or through a Facebook group, or take a course. Let your intuition show you who and where to go to.

2. Start now, before the crisis, to look for who you would approach if you needed help when an emergency arose. Use Google, groups, books and your own intuition – see who you're drawn to. Have them do a communication with your animal so you can see how they work and if you can "take" what they say. If they are professional, they will almost certainly charge a fee. Some may specialise in behaviour problems, lost animals or end of life work. Go with what feels right to you.

And if what feels right to you is none of the above, that's fine too. We all have our own paths, and all are valid. These are just suggestions for those who might find them helpful.

Wishing you love, joy and a forever connection with the animals you have the privilege of sharing your life with,

Sue and Elaine.

Email: animalmatters@aol.com
www.animalcommunication.co.uk
www.petlossoasis.com

Animal Matters *in the Media*

Pet L♥ss Oasis
Nurturing the heart and soul of people grieving animals

Veterinary Botanicals

Canine 'Distemper' Resurgence

Cynthia Lankenau, DVM, CVA, RH (AHG)

9002 Sunset Drive, Colden, NY 14033

Canine distemper is highly contagious viral disease of dogs and other members of the Canidae family; caused by a single-stranded RNA virus; a paramyxovirus. The disease has a worldwide occurrence and is often characterized by severe clinical disease. (Farrow, 1980) The initial infection is characterized by temperature elevation, transient anorexia, depression, and mild serous conjunctivitis. In dogs that fail to develop an adequate immune response, the virus can spread rapidly to the epithelial cells and the central nervous system. There is considerable evidence that Canine Distemper can cause immuno-suppression. (Farrow, 1980) Due to the use of vaccination, over the past few decades, this disease has not been commonly seen in the general population.

Recently there has been a resurgence of this deadly disease concentrated in populations of shelter dogs. In general, these abandoned dogs are in a poor nutritional state when rescued. These dogs upon arrival into a rescue facility generally receive a full complement of vaccines with the intention to protect the animals from these diseases including Distemper/Hepatitis/Parainfluenza/Leptospirosis/Parvo and Rabies while also receiving topical flea products, oral wormers. Usually within a few days if intact, these animals are neutered.

Case:

'Bean' is a mastiff cross who was picked up as a stray on May 22, 2015. On May 29, she was vaccinated with a four way Leptospirosis vaccine, Parainfluenza/ Bordetalla, Distemper/Hepatitis/Parvo/Parainfluenza and Rabies and was treated chemically for external parasites and internal parasites with pyrantel pamoate (Strongid). She additionally was surgically neutered with an ovario-hysterectomy and released for adoption on May 30. Her new owner noted immediately the presence of a moderately severe conjunctivitis. By the June 1, 2015, Bean had become very lethargic with a very poor appetite and was examined.

Signs and symptoms:

On June 1, 2015; Bean was found to have a significant conjunctivitis with a serous bilateral ocular discharge; she had a 105 degree F temperature. She had bilateral rales throughout her lung lobes, but with large areas in the ventral quadrates with no auscultable air flow, and felt to be areas of pulmonary consolidation; a mucoid nasal discharge with significant respiratory distress. She was extremely thin

From her physical exam, she was diagnosed with pneumonia and conjunctivitis, presumed to be caused by Canine Distemper.

Western diagnostics: Radiographs confirmed pneumonia

Treatment goals:

- To improve immune function to regain health and vitality: immunomodulating, adaptogens

- To improve respiratory function: antimicrobial, antiviral, antiseptic, expectorant, bronchodilatant, anticatarrhal, diuretic.

- To improve appetite and improve digestive functions: digestive bitters, Hepatotrophorestoratives

Herbal Prescription: Equal parts of:

- Echinacea, *Echinacea angustifolia;*

- Lomatium, *Lomatium dissectum;*

- Andrographis, *Andrographis paniculata* ;

- St. John's Wort, *Hypericum perforatum;*

- Mullein leaf, *Verbascum thapsus*; and

- ¼ Blood Root, *Sanguinaria canadensis*

in a 1:3 tincture; 10 drops hourly for the initial doses

Echinacea, *Echinacea angustifolia;* Echinacea is an antimicrobial, anti-inflammatory, alternative immunoregulator and tonic herb with anticatarrhal effects. It is considered by many to have adaptogenic qualities. Felter and Lloyd considered it to be an important herb in toxic states that have septicemia. Energetically it clears heat toxins that can cause septicemia. It has been proven to be effective in acute or chronic bacterial or viral respiratory conditions. Knowing that Distemper often creates neurologic symptoms, Professor Webster stated that Echinacea has action is slow forms of cerebromeningitis and that it acts as a stimulant to the capillary circulation and that no remedy is comparable with it. (Felter and Lloyd, 1983)

Mullein leaf, *Verbascum thapsus* is a relaxing expectorant, mild diuretic, mucilaginous. It is valuable for all lung problems because it nourishes as well as strengthens, it promotes expectoration and resolves viscous Lung phlegm and relieves coughing; it opens the chest and relieves wheezing, and can reduce allergy; it clears damp heat; and clears Fire toxins, removes lymph congestion,. (Holmes, 1994) It has been used to treat asthma, pleurisy, pneumonia, croup, tracheitis, emphysema, tuberculosis, contagious bronchitis.   In deep respiratory cases, it helps remove the phlegm deep in the airways while reducing allergic reactions and allows the deeper airways to open. Mullein polyphenols play an important role in exerting the antioxidant effect; anti-inflammatory activity is correlated to iridoids and phenylethanoids.

***Andrographis paniculata,* Andrographis** is an immunomodulation, antimicrobial, hepatoprotective, bitter tonic that has antibacterial, antipyretic, anti-inflammatory effects; antimalarial, with cardiovascular effects; antiplatelet and antithrombotic activity. It is hepatoprotective and an antihepatotoxin. It has a cholagogic, choleretic effect that can help the liver produce and move more bile to assist in detoxification of the systemic inflammatory products. It traditionally is also used as a tonic and restorative in convalescence. Energetically it Clears Heat and Eliminates Toxins; and Dries up Damp which was a newer symptom. It is indicated in upper respiratory tract infections, Cough, sore throat; Liver disease. The herb is traditionally given as a restorative and tonic in convalescence giving non-specific immune stimulant, hepatoprotectant. Current research has seen it to be protective and preventative respiratory infections.

***Lomatium dissectum* Lomatium, Biscuitroot**: Lomatium is antiseptic, disinfectant, pectoral, salve, stomachic and tonic; antiviral, antimicrobial, immunostimulant, adaptogen. Lomatium first attracted the attention of the medical community when it was shown to be effected in treatment an influenza epidemic in the Great Basin area during the 1920's When influenza hit Nevada and New Mexico (1920-22) it wiped out whole villages of tough Shoshone and New Mexican mountain folks. After some experimenting, in Nevada and eastern Oregon, the herb of choice, from Oregon Trailers to Jack Mormons to Shoshone, was Leptotaenia Root (Now called *Lomatium dissectum*), and Great Basin pharmacies widely

A picture of St. John's Wort

sold the tincture and Indians and settlers and ranchers and cowboys passed the dried root around. (Moore, 2003) It is a powerful antiviral/antibacterial agent, it is being used to reduce viral load in chronic conditions. It is an active pulmonary antiseptic. (Winston, 2009) This is an endangered herb. ONLY use this herb is harvested from a sustainable source.

St. John's Wort, *Hypericum perforatum,* has been used traditionally as a pectoral (Levy, 1988), its use in respiratory catarrh (Grieve, 1971), and it ability to soothe irritated nerves with the recent research of its ability to kill paramyxoviruses such as the species responsible for Canine Distemper.

Picture of Bloodroot; medicinally the root is used. This is an at risk herb, do not wild harvest but purchase from a sustainable source.

Bloodroot, *Sanguinaria canadensis* was felt in this case, to be of critical importance due to the areas of consolidated pulmonary tissue. It is an expectorant, antispasmodic, cardiotonic, diuretic, sedative, anticatarrhal, circulatory stimulant, bitter hepatobiliary tonic, cholagogue. The specific indication is Hepatization of the lung (Ellington, 1919) while it promotes expectoration, resolves viscous phlegm, relieves coughing and will help to removes pulmonary accumulation. It has been traditionally used for convalescence from pneumonia with exhaustion and coughing; indicated in severe, chronic bronchial, hepatic conditions presenting as a deficiency, cold with phlegm and mucus discharges. The alkaloids, sanguinarine and chelerythrine, are felt to be bio-active. (Ross, 2010) Fyfe also states that often for coughs, "it is absolutely necessary to continue the drug for a considerable period of time. Dose is important, In minute doses we employ it in cases of cough with dryness of the throat and air passages, feeling of constriction in the chest, difficult and asthmatic breathing with sensation of pressure. In the same dose it is a stimulant to the vegetative system of nerves and under its use there is an improvement in the circulation, in nutrition and secretion." Research has shown Bloodroot extracts having potential as therapeutic immunomodulators, and has been shown to inhibit platelet aggregation. No known drug interactions.

Picture taken June 7, 2015; note the emaciated condition of Bean; she often needed to stand in this posture in order to breathe.

Advice given:

Follow up:

Started with Echinacea, Lomatium, Andrographis, St. John's Wort, Mullein leaf; equal parts with 1/4 part Blood Root. She is a mastiff cross; and had the owner give 10 drops hourly, to start; as she also was very anorexic and did not want to upset her stomach. Over the next three days, she started eating, temperature returned to normal; she was still breathing fast though but rales were decreased; but changed to 40 drops four times a day.

June 7, 2015: lungs sound normal-stopped the Blood root but maintained dose at 40 drops four times a day.

Taken on June 20, 2015; resting, comfortable with appreciable weight gain.

June 14, 2015 she seems OK, no neurological signs; but keeping her on St. John's Wort, Echinacea, Andrographis, and Mullein.

June 29, 2015: She is acting great, plan to slowly wean off her herbs

Reflections: Canine Distemper is a highly fatal disease. Bean was critically ill and needed professional care. In her case, her veterinary herbal therapy was crucial to her safe and speedy recovery. There is no drug available with the anti-viral, adaptogenic, anticatarrhal, pulmonary circulatory normalizers, antimicrobial, antiseptic, expectorant, bronchodilatant, anticatarrhal, diuretic; and digestive bitter effects that are present in this bouquet of herbal medicines.

The question to be asked is whether the immunosuppression from her Distemper and Parvo vaccination while in a poor nutritional and stressed state was responsible for the manifestation of the active Canine Distemper?

Cynthia is a mixed animal practitioner in western New York who has a specialty practice using only alternative modalities and is a member and currently past-president of the VBMA.

References:

1. Ellington, F., 1919; American Materia Medica, Therapeutics and Pharmacognosy: Eclectic Medical Publications; Sandy Oregon, p. 242-3.

2. Farrow, B, 1980; Canine Distemper, Current Veterinary Therapy VII, Saunders Company; p.1284-1286.

3. Felter and Lloyd, 1983; King's American Dispensatory, vol 1; Eclectic Medical Publications, Sandy, Oregon; p. 671-677.

4. Grieve, M., 1971; A Modern Herbal, vol. II; Dover Publications, NY, p. 707-708

5. Holmes, P; 1994; The Energetics of Western Herbs, Vol. II; Snow Lotus, Boulder, CO; p.480.

6. Levy, J., 1988; The Complete Herbal Handbook for Farm and Stable; Faber and Faber, London, 138-9.

7. Moore, M., 2003, Medicinal Plants of the Mountain West, Museum of New Mexico Press.

8. Ross, J, 2010; Combining Western Herbs and Chinese Medicine: A Clinical Materia Medica; Greenfields Press, Regensburg, Germany.

9. Winston, D., 2009; Herbal Therapeutics; Herbal Therapeutics Research Library, Broadway, N.J. p. 105

Homeopathy in a case of skin fold pyoderma

Susan Andreseir

Homeopathy was originally the work of an 18th century physician called Samuel Hahnemann. He wondered why Peruvian tree bark was effective in treating some of the symptoms of swamp fever (now known as Malaria). He took some of the tree bark himself (even though he had no symptoms of swamp fever) and developed the symptoms of swamp fever. From this the principle of 'like cures like' was formulated.

Many of the treatments for disease at this time were highly toxic and had very unpleasant, sometimes fatal side effects, so Hahnemann set about trying to find the lowest possible effective doses of commonly used medications. Hahnemann found that if he diluted the substance and at each dilution vigorously shook the mixture in a specific way (called succussion) they were still highly effective without any of the unpleasant side effects.

Homeopathy involves finding the correct 'patient picture' and matching it as closely as possible to the correct 'remedy picture' therefore helping the body to heal itself. When using homeopathy to treat a case, I look at the whole animal and its' environment, and as well as prescribing a remedy, I often advise changes to the animals diet, routine etc. that will benefit the animal. I always like to work closely with the animals first opinion vet and alongside any conventional therapies or medications that they may be taking.

Danni

Although this photography does not show it very well, Danni had been suffering for many years from facial skin fold dermatitis. This is a notoriously difficult condition to treat, both conventionally and non-conventionally.

When I first saw Danni he was nine years old and had suffered from this condition since he was about two. Over the years he had had numerous courses of antibiotics, steroids, topical creams and washes, and had even had corrective surgery, effectively giving him a 'face lift'. Sadly none of these treatments had provided significant relief for him and at the time of my first consultation Dannis' owner was applying a strong steroid cream prescribed for human use. His owner reported that he was intensely irritated by his condition, frequently rubbing his face along the edges of furniture and carpets, and leaving brown marks everywhere. The skin within the folds was highly inflamed, had copious discharge and crusting, as well as a strong unpleasant odour. The skin around his facial folds had become hairless. After taking his history it became apparent that nothing in particular made his condition worse or better, he was fed a commercially available dog food, as well as small amounts of cheese. He came to live with his current owners at about 19 months of age, he was vaccinated, neutered and then had a traumatic incident, that resulted in temporary impairment of the use f his hind legs, which he made a full recovery from. Soon after this period his face flared up and had been a problem ever since.

Often in homeopathy we are looking for the strange and peculiar symptoms, that are specific to that particular animal, so that we can find the best fitting remedy. However, in Dannis' case, I decided initially to treat him using his local symptoms, as he had had the condition for so long and there were abundant local signs, as well as a lack of deep emotional symptoms. The best fitting local remedy was Graphites and I prescribed a twice daily dose at 6c potency. This was dispensed in liquid form and dropped on to the tongue. I also advised that the steroid cream be discontinued and that twice daily cleansing with Dermocent pyo-clean wipes and Atop-7 (based on natural ingredients including caper flower bud extract, essential fatty acids, essential oils of cajputi and tea tree) applied to cotton wool and then onto the affected area could be beneficial. I also advised cutting cheese out of his diet.

After four weeks I examined him again and he had significantly improved, however some crusting and inflammation was still evident and he had developed black wart like deposits on his tongue and face. Taking into account his history and new symptoms, I prescribed a split dose of Thuja 30c and advised continuation with the Graphites and cleaning regime.

Again I re-examined him in four weeks and his owner reported that his condition had become transiently worsened after the Thuja (a temporary worsening of the condition can sometimes occur in homeopathy) followed by a good improvement. Dannis' owner reported that he resented being cleaning with the pyo-clean wipes and sometimes his skin would appear more inflamed after cleaning, so we decided to discontinue the wipes, but continue with the Atop 7 and Graphites remedy.

When I next saw him, the skin within the facial folds was a healthy pink, with some hair regrowth, he had no significant crusting or discharge and the black warty deposits were gone. His owner reported that he no longer rubbed his face along the furniture or carpets. Initially I advised twice weekly cleaning and Graphites and then on an as needed basis.

Danni continues to require occasional cleaning and administration of Graphites remedy, but his condition has vastly improved and he is a much happier little dog.

References

Saxton J, Gregory P. Textbook of Veterinary Homeopathy: Beaconsfield; 2005

Gregory P. Insights into Veterinary Homeopathy: Saltaire; 2013

Susan qualified from the Royal Veterinary College in 2002 and worked in general practice for 10 years. She trained in acupuncture with the Association of Veterinary Acupuncturists (ABVA) in 2007 and has also trained in electroacupuncture.

In 2012 Susan founded Acupaws. In addition to running her own practice she has been busy training in both veterinary herbal medicine and veterinary homeopathy. She has completed two years of study at the Bristol

school of homeopathy and gained the qualification of LFHom(vet). Susan is a member of the Royal college of Veterinary Surgeons (RCVS), the Association of British Veterinary Acupuncturists (ABVA), the British Association of Homeopathic Veterinary Surgeons (BHVS), and is an active member on the committee of the British Association of Veterinary Herbalists (BAVH).

"I feel honoured to be able to treat and help my patients. Many of them come to me either unable to take conventional medications due to side effects, pre-existing medical conditions or often as their condition progresses conventional medications have become less effective. It is so rewarding to see them enjoying their lives again."

www.acupaws.co.uk

N.B. This is a great example of the use of homeopathy in treating a bacterial/yeast infection when the pet is on a kibble/dried diet.

The nutritionists at Healthful Dog would suggest that converting a dog with a such a skin infection on to a species appropriate raw diet, would yield a faster result.

Research has shown that the simple carbohydrates found in kibble turn to sugar in the system and feed such infections, whilst also negatively effecting digestion and therefore immunity.

Whilst every patient is unique, a balanced raw diet, devoid of simple carbs, with the addition of nutraceuticals that would support the immune system, pre and pro-biotics and a natural anti-bacterial and anti-fungal, has been shown to clear similar skin conditions within weeks.

Owner Odyssey

Rodney Habib

Here's the truth, I destroyed my best friend with my lack of education, with my ignorance. I destroyed my first pet with my own hands. I laid in a puddle of blood with him after the melamine scandal and I wasn't really the same after that.

Then, only less than a year later in 2008 I got my first puppy.... she was everything that was ever important to me. It was between me and a family who were light years ahead of me with knowledge and as selfish as I was at that time, I convinced the breeder to let me have her. Two months later, I had stuffed her with so many chicken jerky strips I destroyed her kidneys as a puppy, permanently. She will never be the same again because of me. I ruined a beautiful creature of God with my own hands, again.

> So I made a promise to her and God that I would never EVER make that mistake again!

I started teaching myself, researching day and night and trying to tell people about it. I can't write, I can't read very well either, but I had to learn, so I started writing for her, my pup Sammie.

Sounds like a cheesy corny story I know, but today, after 6 years, she still lays beside me as I write and I do it for her. She has a kidney at 25% function and a body full of tumours. Nothing on this planet can inspire one more than that.

> In 2 years, I have achieved things I couldn't possibly imagine!

I'm at two time award winning blogger (who can't write), I had the number one radio show in Canada, which I left as I had been offered a role on Animal Planet to film a TV show for them for 2016.

I get to write for the largest pet nutrition magazine on the planet and I do a zillion other things.

I tell every single one of them the same thing:

> **Give me a stage and let me share my message — that's all I ask.**

I do it for the cat I destroyed who looks down on me in heaven and for the dog that lays beside me full of cancer.

facebook.com/RodneyHabib

facebook.com/PlanetPawsPetEssentials

N.B. Rodney Habib is a genuine Canine SuperHero, please follow him on Facebook and share his blogs to educate all other pet owners and help improve global pet health.

Natural Breeders Register

If you are looking for a new pet, or to re-home a pet, but want it to have come from or go to a raw feeding, non-chemically treated source, then try the Natural Breeders Register.

NBR

Facebook.com/groups/
NaturalBreedersRegisterUK

Copy Dates - 2014/2015

31st October 2015

31st January 2016

30th April 2016

31st July 2016

All articles, letters to the editor and fully formatted adverts are to be submitted at no later than the above dates for each next edition.

Send attached articles, photographs and .pdfs to :

contact@healthful.uk.com

Recommended Natural Therapists

Some therapies that we have investigated are certainly worth bearing in mind when certain circumstances arise with your pet, however due to a number of unethical, untrained, cowboys out there, that may not help your pet one bit and could potentially even make them worse, we recommend finding a practitioner via an association or regulatory body. Here are some of the therapies and associated regulatory bodies we recommend:

Acupuncture	www.abva.co.uk
Bowen	www.bowen-technique.com
Herbalist	www.herbalvets.org.uk
	www.vbma.org
Homeopathy	www.bahvs.com
	www.ahvma.org
Hydrotherapy	www.narch.org.uk
McTimoney	www.mctimoney-animal.org.uk
Physiotherapy	www.acpat.org
Reiki	www.reikifed.co.uk
Tellington Touch	www.ttouchteam.co.uk

Also any ANNAHP Registered therapist and all Wagdale practitioners.

www.annahp.co.uk   www.wagdale.org.uk

Pumpkin: Scary or Sweet?

H B Turner

For some reason I've always had an uncomfortable/irrational negative feeling when people recommend pumpkin or any other of the myriad of varieties of squash, and I have avoided feeding them, or even eating them myself, other than the odd courgette.

Upon further investigation is appears that the calcium to phosphorous ratio within them is not optimum for the use of the body, recommendations being 1:1 or technically 1:0.8 (AAFCO) and squash being closer to 1:2. However recommendations for laboratory animals are between 2:1 & 1:2, as long as Vitamin D levels are high enough, so this shouldn't be a problem right?

Pumpkin contains high amounts of both alpha and beta carotene, known to boost immune function in older dogs and with side effects of too much being Carotenemia (skin discolouration), known to be harmless. Pumpkin has over 8,500 i.u. of Vitamin A per 100g (USDA), with recommendations being around 5,000 i.u. and a maximum of 250,000 i.u. (AAFCO) how could this be a risk?

These recommendations are per units per kilogram, not of dogs, but of substance fed, meaning the 8,500 i.u. per 100g of pumpkin, translates to 85,000 i.u. per kilo, within tolerance, but 15 times the daily recommendation.

O.K. so what does that mean?

A Calcium/Phosphate ratio of 1:2, even when providing bones with a ratio of 1:1, cannot be majorly altered, this can lead to increased calcium levels in the blood (hypercalcemia), this can:

- weaken bones
  ◊ causing bone pain and muscle weakness
- create kidney stones
  ◊ also causing excessive thirst frequent urination
- Effect digestion
  ◊ stomach upset, nausea, vomiting, constipation
- interfere with brain function
  ◊ causing confusion, lethargy and fatigue
- effect heart function

Excess quantities of Vitamin A (hypervitaminosis) can lead to:

- Bone Hypertrophy (bone growths)
- Ankylosing Spondylosis (bone fusion) of the cervical vertebrae
- Effects foetal brain and eye development
- Congenital birth defects - malformations of the eye, skull, lungs & heart
- Increased inter-cranial pressure (pseudotumor cerebri)
- Dizziness
- Nausea
- Headaches
- Skin Irritation
- Pain in Joints and Bones
- Coma
- Death

Prognosis - Guarded to poor due to irreversible liver damage

It also:

- reduces bone mineral density
- increases fracture risk

Long term high Vitamin A consumption is associated with an increased risk of:

- lung cancer
- ischemic heart disease
- cardiovascular disease mortality (National Institute of Health)

Kidney damage and aging increase the risk of toxicity, levels of chronic toxicity in people are at 50,000 i.u. per day

These excesses are usually caused by too much liver, rather than coming from vegetable sources, however an important other issue with excess amounts of Vitamin A is that it interferes with Vitamin D absorption, adding to the issue caused by the calcium/phosphorous imbalance, contrary to recommendations and leading to bone loss.

Therefore, with the combination of both the calcium/phosphate imbalance, the high amount of Vitamin A , the fact that pumpkin/squash are high in starch (48.3%), which negates protein digestion (see How Starch Negates Proteins), and has a high Glycemic Index (75); I can now personally justify my natural reluctance to feed pumpkin and other squashes. With many companies adding pumpkin and squash into their recipes and a number of nutritionists recommending it as a nutrient source, you the reader must make your own decision.

The Natural Dog Conference

Saturday 4th & Sunday 5th December

Birmingham

Speaker Lineup:

Rodney Habib
Pet Nutrition Blogger

Dr Karen Becker
Integrative Pet Care Expert

Dr Jean Dodds
Founder of Hemopet

Dr Nick Thompson
Holistic Veterinarian

Dr Sue Armstrong
Veterinary Surgeon & Homeopath

Caroline Ingram
Founder of Applied Zoopharmacognosy

Dr Isla Fishburn
Holistic Dog Behaviourist

Caroline Griffith
Spiritual Dog Trainer

We the contributors at Healthful Dog are very excited about this conference and cannot wait to meet you there.

For further details go to:

http://naturaldogconference.com/

NURTURE THEM NATURALLY

RAW FOOD SPECIALISTS

2 DARTMOUTH COURT,
GOSPORT, HAMPSHIRE,
PO14 4EW
02392 177271

NURTURETHEMNATURALLY.CO.UK

Naturally Healthy Dogs

Raw Food Deliveries across

East Anglia

07590 621636

www.NaturallyHealthyDogs.co.uk

Healthful

Healthful Pet Mince

Shown to increase health and longevity and reduce veterinary bills. Enjoyed by dogs & wolves.

Also available from Healthful:

Fridays' Dogs Body Herbals

Aloe Products

De-Dog It Natural cleaning products

Medi-tag

contact@healthful.uk.com

www.healthful.uk.com

Product Review

Canine and Feline synthetic pheromone sprays & plug-ins

H B Turner

These products are generally recommended by veterinarians and/or behaviourists and therefore owners invest. Their purpose is in general to calm the animal down and whilst a number of owners swear by them, in general they cannot seem to put their finger on how it has helped. There are also a great number of owners who have bought these products and found that it did not appear to make any difference and therefore discontinued use. We are also aware of rescue centers who use them in kennels and wouldn't consider not doing so. So what is it that they do, or are supposed to do?

According to their website the feline product prevents spraying, scratching, loss of appetite, general mischief and hiding behaviours by it's replication of the pheromone (F3) left when cats mark their territory by rubbing 'its nose against objects in the home'.

There is a 'warning' when using the spray, to "Always wait about 15 minutes before letting your cat near any sprayed areas."

Ingredients:

- F3 hormone 2%
- Ethanol >80%
    (Teratogen, group 1 carcinogen, addictive)
- Pimelic acid <5%
    (Either made from Cyclohexanone—moderately toxic, vapour is an irritant, linked with decreased heart function, swelling, loss of taste and short term memory loss, or made from Salicylic Acid— known for it's major function in aspirin, particularly toxic to cats)
- Azelaic acid <5%
    (Derived from wheat, rye & barley, traditionally used to treat acne, decreases keratin production which may effect claw growth and strength, as well as skin & fur)

Warnings:

- Highly flammable (both liquid and vapour)
- Causes serious eye irritation
- May cause skin irritation
- May cause respiratory irritation
- Dispose of contents at hazardous waste points

The canine version contains "the pheromone that bitches produce whilst lactating to help bond with their puppies". These are available in spray and plug-in form as well as in collars.

Ingredients:

- Isopropanol >50% (Rubbing alcohol, skin irritant, central nervous system depressant)
    (no other ingredients listed)

Warnings:

- Highly flammable (both liquid and vapour)
- Causes serious eye irritation
- May cause drowsiness or dizziness
- Avoid breathing vapours
- Dispose of contents at hazardous waste points

Given that only half of the ingredients are listed on the canine product, the warnings and risks associated with the ingredients that are listed on both products, we would highly recommend that you seek alternative options prior to resorting to these product.

Sources: www.feliway.com
www.ceva.us/content/download/47825/940759/version/1/file/MSDS Feliway Spray_V5.0pdf
www.ceva.us/content/download/47822/940747/version/1/file/MDSD Adaptil Spray_US_V2.0.pdf
http://www.petmd.com/cat/conditions/digestive/c_ct_aspirin_tox

The use of TTouch with Severe Behavioural Problems

Julie Moss

BSc Hons, AdvCertVPhys, Dip.APhys, P1. MIRVAP

I feel TTouch is often dismissed or overlooked as an animal therapy, purely because of its simplicity. The movements are tiny and the exercises simple and I think many people feel that nothing could poly have happened as a result of this work to change their dog, even when the results speak for themselves.

However, I believe it is this very simplicity which is the key to its effectiveness. A little goes a long way and it is possible to make huge changes to dogs in just one session. This can be very useful for clients who would struggle with complicated training programmes and who need to see that things an changing order to rebuild the relationship with their dog. Of course not all problems can be changed overnight and there will always be an element of training or management included in a therapy programme, but TTouch can provide an accessible way for a client to reconnect with their dog and begin the process.

Another mistaken belief is that TTouch can only help with simple or mild behavioural problems. Even severe behavioural cases can have a remarkable turnaround with just one or two sessions of TTouch and I vividly remember one particularly severe case, many years ago where TTouch was just the thing needed for the dog and client to move forward, and even now, I can't think of anything else which would have given such rapid and stunning results.

The Story of Sammy and Gerald

One afternoon I received a call from the local rescue centre, to say a man had tried to hand his dog over because h was so terrified he couldn't be left alone, wouldn't go out and was toileting indoors. The dog was his best friend in the world and he couldn't cope with seeing him like that, but also couldn't bear to put him to sleep. He was in a horrible and desperate situation. I was given his details and asked to contact him to see if I could help, so I gave him a call.

Gerald sounded OK on the phone and told me about his dog Sammy, who had previously been his gun dog when he went out on shoots as a hobby. Sammy loved his work and everything was fine until Gerald had to go into hospital eight months earlier. Sammy went to stay with a gamekeeper, who let him roam outside on the vast estate for the week that Gerald was in hospital. Gerald came home to find Sammy deeply traumatised from this experience and now, months later, he was extremely withdrawn, wouldn't play or go out, didn't interact with anyone and Gerald was both devastated and desperate.

I decided I should probably see him that day, so packed a bag and travelled to see him. On the way I was wondering just where I was going to start. There were several issues and they had been going on for eight months. On top of that I had a desperate owner, who was at the end of his tether.

- Would Sammy be able to come out and work with me?

- Did I have time to do enough to help them stay together?

I had lots of doubts, but it is always worth trying.

I arrived to meet a very anxious Gerald who ushered me into the house and pointed to a dark shape under the table at the back of the room. I could just about make out that it was a black Labrador hiding away as far back as he could be. I asked Gerald to make us both a cup of tea so we could sit and have a chat. I sat on the floor at the front of the room as we talked.

During the conversation Sammy came out from under the table and sat quivering just within reach of me. He sniffed my arm and I held out a hand to him, which he tentatively sniffed. I stroked his shoulder with the back of my hand and he moved nearer.

I started to do some very gentle TTouches wherever he was comfortable and he immediately leaned on me. I continued and he practically threw himself on the floor to receive more.

At this point Gerald's jaw had pretty much also hit the floor, because usually

Sammy would run away from visitors and go back under the table, if indeed he ever managed to come out at all!

I have to say I don't think I have ever met a dog more ready to receive help than Sammy. Touching him was like touching a wooden statue; he was so tense and tight. He soaked up the TTouch work like a sponge and just lay there grunting and stretching. I could feel the tension begin to drain from him as his body softened and he began to relax for the first time in months. Gerald was close to tears actually so was I.

This all occurred within the first forty-five minutes of visit. It was incredibly fast progress. Sammy was now also wearing a body wrap and was snoring. I continued to alternate between work with him and giving him breaks as Gerald was telling me stories about himself and Sammy, and what they used to get up to.

There came a point where Sammy suddenly stood up, wagged his tail and began to look around. I asked Gerald what his favourite toy was and he handed me a very dusty ball, which obviously hadn't been played with in some time. Sammys' eyes lit up as I rolled it along the floor. Then he pounced and carried it to Gerald who was delighted. They began to play a gentle game of ball together in the room and I suggested Sammy might like a drink and to go outside. He did both eagerly and with no trace of apprehension. At this point I was probably as amazed Gerald at the speed of Sammys' progress. This was a severely troubled dog and yet he was almost back to the dog he had been eight months ago.

I stayed a while longer to make sure things were set to continue and advised Gerald to have some fun with Sammy and remind him of all the fun things they once did together. I showed him how to do just a couple of touches, left him a body wrap and prepared to leave. As I stood up, he took hold of my hands, looked me the eye and said 'Thank you. You really have no idea what you've done'. I will never forget how happy they both looked, as if they were having a reunion and rediscovering each other after being separated for a very long time. I will always feel so pleased I could enable them to stay together and be happy.

At lunchtime the following day Gerald phoned me to say he and Sammy had just got up! Apparently Sammy had slept right through the night for the first time since his ordeal. They had got up earlier, had a quick wander outside, then gone back to bed again for more sleep—just because they could!

So sometimes you don't need very much to kick start the healing process. You just need the right thing for t dog, delivered in the right way. TTouch is so gentle, flexible an non-prescriptive it can do that. Simply asking the dog what they need right now and giving it, can negate the need for lengthy complicated processes, because if the first step is in place, they often do the rest themselves. Even if a dog can't be touched, we can work through their person or use groundwork exercises.

(Names have been changed and the photographed dogs are Evie, Jax andFizzie)

Want to know more?

I offer one to one TTouch sessions and workshops as do many other practitioners around the country if you need one local to you. For other practitioners and more information go to www.ttouch.co.uk

Julie Moss *BSc Hons, AdvCertVPhys, Dip.APhys, P1. MIRVAP.*

www.bestbehaviouranimaltherapy.co.uk

https://www.facebook.com/bestbehaviouranimaltherapy

Best Behaviour
Animal Therapy
Behavioural and Physical Rehabilitation

Save a dog – help a veteran & improve the lives of both, for military & emergency services veterans with PTSD

Service Dogs UK aims to provide veterans from the Armed Forces and Emergency Services, who are suffering with Post-traumatic stress disorder (PTSD), the benefit of specially trained assistance dogs from rescue. We will train dogs to the highest standard with the goal of achieving Assistance Dogs International accreditation, meaning they will have public access and can be with the veteran at all times.

It is easy to forget, that those who serve on the frontline, be it at home or abroad, often see and experience awful things so that you and I do not have to. But this bravery does come at a cost for some and they need your support! PTSD is the brain's response to an extremely traumatic experience or experiences, assistance dogs can help people cope with this disabling condition.

For those in the armed forces it is often triggered by being in combat. For those in the emergency services it is can be triggered by life-threatening experiences, having to deal with horrific road side accidents or child abuse cases.

People who suffer with PTSD can have various symptoms that makes life difficult and disabling - just because you cannot see the injury doesn't mean it's not there. Typically, sufferers will experience or feel anger, grief, flashbacks, guilt, despair, depression, emotional numbness, sleeplessness, loss of trust, fear, work/family problems and suicidal thoughts. **Dogs can really help!**

Dogs are able to 'draw out' even the most isolated people. Through engaging with a dog, veterans are able to overcome emotional numbness and lower social barriers; it is much easier to talk about dogs than it is about yourself! Through training a dog, veterans develop new ways to communicate without anger or fear.

What trained dogs can do

Practical things like fetching items and other "classical" assistance dog tasks to other tasks that help someone with PTSD. Our dogs will also be trained in more 'specific' tasks for the particular veteran such as;

- Dogs wake you, nudge, lick & calm you.
- Dogs give a non-judgemental friendship and comfort.
- Bonding with a dog releases the hormone oxytocin in the brain which impacts positively on trusting and empathy abilities - allowing for a sufferer to engage more in social activity.
- Dogs can recognise stress and anxiety and can redirect the person to more positive activities.

Why rescue dogs

We feel that our veterans will have an empathy with rescue dogs. They know what it is like to be in a difficult and sometimes desperate situation. Now, they can change a dog's life for the better and change their own lives at the same time. Doing something positive is very powerful feeling! Rescue dogs, like veterans with PTSD, have their 'battle' scars and being able to help each other empowers both.

You can make the difference!

We rely on public donations to make a difference and to help those who need it most. We are a voluntary organisation, always on the look out for helpers such as; trainers, fosterers and volunteers. We want you to be inspired! So... Start preparing for that marathon, organise a dog walk or coffee morning, sell delicious cup cakes, or anything else that takes your fancy to help us raise much needed funds!

If that all sounds too tricky, that's OK, a donation will go a long way too.

Donations & Find Out More: ServiceDogsUK.org

DOGA UNLEASHED

Amy Stevens' developed an exercise programme, where you do yoga with your dog. Her mission is to not only create a unique situation in which you can grow a deeper relationship with your dog, while both becoming healthier than ever before, but to also donate proceeds of sales to animal related charities. DU wants to ensure that world wide, we are in fact making a difference in the lives of those without a voice of their own.

How does my dog actually do yoga?

This workout is primarily focused on people doing yoga to increase their overall health and well-being while including dogs into the routine. You will be the one doing most of the work as you intermittently give your dog basic training commands, stretch them out, administer massages and ultimately spend quality time with your pup, improving your relationship. Soon after starting the Doga Unleashed DVD workouts you will not only see your energy, sleeping patterns and over all health enhancing, but you will also notice the same types of progress in your dog as well!

How will I know if my dog is able to participate in a Dog Yoga workout?

We strongly advise that you have your dog(s) health inspected by a licensed veterinarian before starting any new exercise routines. Please note: your dog may be a little reluctant at first, think of the yoga workout as a new training tool. It will take time and patience for you both to learn the routine, become comfortable with it and for your pup to fully engage and focus. Don't worry, after a couple of weeks with consistent practice, you'll both be Doga pros in no time!

http://www.dogaunleashed.com/

Spotlight on....
Does kitty litter contain harmful substances?

Jessica Grillo

Perhaps there is more to fear from kitty litter than just the unpleasantness of the daily clean out. The most common cat litters contain ingredients proven to be harmful when exposed to humans and animals. The use of sodium bentonite clay and silica gel in litters coupled with the threat of aflatoxins in grain based cat litters calls for discretion when purchasing this common household item.

Not to be confused with beneficial calcium bentonite clay non-biodegradable sodium bentonite clay can be harmful if ingested. Sodium bentonite clay contains high levels of sodium ions which have a higher hydration sphere than calcium ions. Sodium bentonite therefore absorbs moisture much better than its calcium counterpart and when wet swells approximately 15 times its original volume. It is because of this factor (and the cheapness of strip-mining the clay) that 50 percent f the litter sold in the U.S. is of the clumping variety and typically made with sodium bentonite clay. The ingestion of super-absorbent sodium bentonite clay by your pets can lead to an accumulation of insoluble masses inside the body causing bowel blockages, kidney problems, dehydration, an inability to absorb nutrients and if left untreated can quickly lead to death.

As an added absorption and deodorizing benefit many kitty litter companies also use silica gel in their formulations. Silica gel is a porous form of silicon dioxide and is made synthetically from a compound called sodium silicate. Silica gel is most commonly found in desiccant packets in newly purchased shoes, electronics or vitamins where excess moisture would encourage the growth of mold or spoilage. Silica gel crystals work as drying agents in kitty litter by trapping cat urine in their small pores while allowing the excess water to evaporate. In 1997, the International Agency for Research on Cancer classified silica as a human carcinogen, yet it is estimated that roughly 95 percent of U.S. cat litter is a form of silica.

Odor isn't the only thing permeating from the litter box

Prolonged exposure to silica dust can pose severe health risks to both animals and humans. Inhalation of silica dust (such as when your pet is frequenting the bathroom or during daily litter box cleanings) can cause irritation and in some cases, permanent damage of the mucous membranes of the lungs and upper respiratory tract, as well as leading to silicosis and lung cancer. As previously mentioned, your pets' natural grooming practices leave them susceptible to ingesting litter and dust that has accumulated over time on their paws and in their hair. Often, kitty litter companies add toxic cobalt(III) chloride to the silica gel when a visible indication of absorption is needed. The cobalt(III) chloride changes from blue to pink when wet and has been directly linked to cancer. Not the best addition to your pets' diet.

So you ditch the toxic soup of clumping silica-based cat litters and opt for a more natural ingredient choice—unfortunately you aren't out of the wood yet. Kitty litter made from grains such as corn or wheat is susceptible to contamination by aflatoxin producing Aspergillus. Grains are particularly susceptible to infection if stored in warm temperatures and moist environments— exactly like your cat litter box. Aflatoxin exposure predominately attacks the liver and can lead to a whole host of serious illnesses.

Protect the health of yourself and your pets by opting for non-clumping and non-toxic kitty litters. Even better, train your cat to use the toilet and forever abolish the need for costly litter, disgusting clean ups and toxin exposure. Not to mention—a cat using a toilet is always a good conversation starter.

Sources for this article include:

http://www.naturalnews.com/035210_bentonite_clay_myths_safety.html

Kathleen E Noone, VMD, ACVIM; Peter L Borchelt, PhD; Cheryl C Rice, DVM; Cindy Bressler, DVM; Jorge Morales, MA; and John J Lee, PhD. Detection of Silica Particles in Lung Wash Fluid from Cats With and Without Respiratory Disease. http://www.google.com

Marina Michaels, Clumping Clay Kitty Litters: A Deadly Convenience? http://thelighthouseonline.com/articles/clump.html

Kapush, Problems with Silica Gel Crystal Cat Litter (October 25th 2011) http://kapush.net/cat-litter/silica-gel-cat-litter-problems/

Silicosis http://en.wikipedia.org/wiki/Silicosis

Aflatoxin http://en.wikipedia.org/wiki/Aflatoxin

Daniela Caride, The best cat litter (March 6 2011) http://taildom.com/blog/reviews/the-best-cat-litter/

Amanda Yarnell, KITTY LITTER: Clay, silica, and plant-derived alternatives compete to keep your cats box clean (April 26 2004) http://pubs.acs.org/cen/whatstuff/stuff/8217kitty.html

Betsy Wild, Silica Gel Packets (August 28 2012) http://betsywild.wordpress.com/tag/silica-gel/

NotEyeSaidTheCat.Wordpress.com

A different cancer treatment - A Case Study

Lissy Seidel
Holistic Vet & Writer

'Your dog has cancer' - this is probably the most emotionally charged sentence you have to deliver to an anxious owner. Reeling from the shock it is understandable that most people would go along with what their vet suggests, she is, after all the experts with the background knowledge to make the best decision.

On second thoughts you as the owner might read through the recommendations and begin to wonder...

This is what happened when Polly's owner sat down and read the comments of the Histologist after a large Mast cell tumour had been removed from her 11 year old Labrador's neck.

Mast cell tumours are very common skin tumours in dogs and are generally classified by degree of differentiation - the poorer the differentiation of the cells, the higher the grade and the worse the prognosis.

Polly's tumour had been growing rapidly and proved impossible to excise with the appropriate skin margins all around; the pathologist's report stated nevertheless that excision had been complete.

All the advanced examinations to determine the stage the cancer had reached had been meticulously carried out and no involvement of liver or spleen been found, nor were there any doubtful areas of shading in abdomen and chest on X-ray.

So - what made the report so alarming then?

The worst factor was the very high mitotic index (indicating a high cell division rate). Polly's tumour showed a mitotic index of 15/10 hpf (15 mitoses observed per 10 high power field) and the threshold for a greater likelihood of metastases and recurrence is under 5. Also her tumour was classified as high grade, so again the outlook for these is much worse as far as treatment and, crucially, survival time goes. Even the risk of local recurrence was considered to be high - further surgery was not really possible due to the location and extent of the original lesion and radiotherapy was recommended at a rate of two to three times weekly for up to 12 treatments.

Quite apart from the generally considerable side effects, the cost of this would have been beyond most insurance plans and certainly a stretch for most people.

Chemotherapy was strongly recommended, the protocol set out a series of treatments lasting between 12 and 18 weeks.

Potential side effects included gastrointestinal signs (nausea, ulceration, spontaneous haemorrhage), low blood pressure, insufficient renal perfusion, disseminated intravascular coagulation (essentially blood clotting within the blood vessels) which carries a risk of sudden death. Last but not least the immune system of the patient is almost inevitably severely compromised.

The histologist's view was that Polly needed chemotherapy as the tumour had a high mitotic rate and the relevant lymph node was highly suspicious for advanced stage disease. He also was anxious to start the treatment without further delay due to the highly aggressive nature of the tumour.

In his summary of the outcome he painted a rather black picture though - he gave Polly a very guarded prognosis (generally I personally interpret these words as 'pretty hopeless') and duly cited various studies that showed that less than 40% of high grade mast cell tumours survive to 1 year post diagnosis and much more significantly the studies of patients with a high mitotic index (over 5/10 hpf) had a mean survival time (MST) of 2 months. These patients had received a variety of treatments, but most had some sort of chemotherapy. Another study that focussed on strict chemotherapy protocol treatments found that grade three patients survived for around 6 months.

The offered disease control time for Polly veered between 2-6 months with chemotherapy. Polly's owner wasn't impressed and decided against any form of chemotherapy - response rates and successful outcomes certainly did not seem to balance out the potentially poor quality of life Polly might experience, not to mention the minuscule chance of remission of her cancer for any reasonable length of time.

Mrs P did some research and found that various dietary recommendations were generally made for canine cancer patients. She contacted me and we arranged for me to meet her and Polly and draw up a treatment plan.

I found Polly in reasonable health and good spirits - thankfully our animals don't share the mental anguish we experience when we ourselves are faced with a major health crisis like that. We talked at length about how to proceed and formulated the following plan:

First and foremost I took Polly off any processed food and any food containing carbohydrates - she was to have a strictly raw meat and raw meaty bones diet. I cautioned against the use of the most palatable vegetables: peas, carrots and parsnips are quite high in sugar and therefore I do not recommend them as a regular addition to the daily diet. I added a freeze dried compound of various vegetables, herbs, nuts and fruits to supply minerals, vitamins and trace elements at an optimal rate.

So far so good, but this was just putting the basics in place, reducing the potential intake of toxic or highly processed components with her daily food.

Vitamin C has been shown to be a vital tool in the fight of cancer cells and I prescribed high doses of Vitamin C for Polly. Now, due to its acidic nature large doses of Vitamin C are not well tolerated and can lead to gastrointestinal problems. One way to avoid that is to give it in liposomal form; the Vitamin C is encapsulated in small globuli of fat, so the stomach lining is protected against any excessive acid and furthermore absorption is greatly enhanced - in fact, with liposomal Vitamin C blood levels can be achieved that are otherwise only possible via intravenous injection.

I also recommended to provide Polly with Glutathione, a powerful antioxidant, again in the liposomal form. Additionally she was fed Curcumin, Bentonite clay and Boron.

Polly took to her new regime like the proverbial duck to water. She loved her new diet and took all the extra bits without a problem.

Additionally her coat improved, her weight stayed stable and she was enjoying her daily walks as much if not more than before.

I got regular updates and everything went very well for around 8 months. Gradually she developed a bit of a cough, though, and then new skin growths appeared in a number of places. She was finally put to sleep 10 months after her diagnosis as she had lost her zest for life and was looking quite mournful.

So was it all worth it?

Had she been subjected to the suggested treatment regime she would have had to endure 4 weeks of radiotherapy followed by 2 courses of chemotherapy lasting 12 and 18 weeks respectively. This adds up to 8 and a half months of heavy duty therapy with likely quite severe side effects and a lot of emotional upheaval due to the need for repeated hospitalisation. Instead she had 9 months of very good quality of life, not to mention the comparatively minute cost of the treatment.

I know what I would choose for my own dog - would you?

HOLISTIC VETERINARY CARE

Tel: 07788 794997
email: lissyacuvet@yahoo.co.uk
web: whatmakesyourhorsetick.co.uk

Introducing Robert Donkers

Robert is a Natural Animal Health Practitioner and new contributor to Healthful Dog.

He has just returned from a gruelling trek around the Great Glen Way from Fort William to Inverness, with his pack of 7 gorgeous dogs, in order to raise funds for

#NoToDogMeat

Dogs are eaten all year round in Korea. In the summer during the hottest periods consumption of dog meat grows into demonic proportions. Thousands and thousands of terrified dogs are slaughtered in the most brutal ways just because the Koreans believe in the ridiculous fallacy that eating of dog meat will help them cope with the hottest temperatures. This is not scientifically substantiated, it is an unfounded belief which has grown into mammoth dimension in Korea.

The first bok nal called "cho bok" is on 15th July the second one called "jung bok" is 25th July and the last one, called "mal bok" is on 14th August On these days, Koreans prepare special food said to strengthen the body during those hot days.

Each year my dogs and I undertake a sponsored trek in the UK to raise money for the No To Dog Meat Foundation.

Why raise money for the No To Dog Meat Foundation?

We strongly believe that it is inherently wrong to eat dog and cat meat. We also believe that the way in which dogs and cats are slaughtered is beyond acceptable human behaviour.

The cruelty and suffering these animals go through is unimaginable. No animal deserves to be boiled alive, skinned alive or any other method of slaughter. Unfortunately many people who keep cats and dogs as pets close their eyes because they can't bear it. However, ignoring the situation makes you complacent and this attitude of denial allows these barbaric practices to continue.

Dogs are humans' best friends. They have helped and continue to help humans in many different situations. Dogs are intelligent animals and fortunately this is very much recognised in the West. Emotionally

dogs (and other animals too) are highly developed. Like us they have a brain and a nervous system. Why do we as humans deny animals these characteristics? Yes, animals can conjure up images of their friends, pack members and owners. Animals physically cry when distressed or in pain, so why allow cruelty?

Help us raise money to stop this cruelty. The No To Dog Meat Foundation works to enforce change of legislation in countries where torturing, killing and eating dogs is practiced.

Check out the NoToDogMeat website:

http://www.notodogmeat.com/

And donate to Roberts cause here:

http://www.totalgiving.co.uk/mypage/robertdonkers

Paleo Cat
Does Your Cat Love Fish?

Celeste Yarnall

If your cat loves fish, he has lots of company!

However, it's really not a good idea to feed fish to your cat; and here's why:

The primary fish used in cat food are salmon, tuna, and tilefish (ocean whitefish). Let's look at each of these.

- Salmon:

The vast majority of salmon today comes from farm-raised fish. In this form of factory farming, millions of these unfortunate animals are kept in huge, overcrowded pens in polluted coastal waters. They're fed antifungals and antibiotics to limit the spread of disease, and dyes to make their flesh salmon-colored (otherwise it would be gray). Common water pollutants, such as PCBs, pesticides, and other chemicals, are found in farmed salmon at ten times the amount found in wild fish. These contaminants will be present in any product made with farmed fish, including pet food. It has recently been revealed that krill, tiny shrimp that are the natural diet of many whales and other marine animals, are being netted in vast hauls, and processed into food for these "franken-salmon," for their protein as well as their red color. The issues with krill are explained below.

- Tuna:

It's the fish that's most "addictive" to cats. They love it so much that they may stage a hunger strike by refusing their regular food until they get it! Tuna and other predatory fish are at the top of the food chain. This means that they may accumulate high levels of heavy metals (including mercury) as well as PCBs, pesticides, and other toxins, by eating smaller fish. The older the fish, the more contamination. Tilefish: (listed on pet food labels as "ocean whitefish") are among the worst contaminated, along with king mackerel, shark, and swordfish. These fish are so toxic that the FDA advises women of child-bearing age and children to avoid them entirely; and the FDA recommends only one serving of albacore tuna per week due to its high mercury levels. The fish used in canned pet foods is typically whole fish, or leftovers from processing whole fish, deemed unsuitable for human consumption; this includes guts, faeces, and bones, which are high in phosphorus—a problem for cats with kidney disease. On the other end of the urinary tract, many sensitive cats develop cystitis (bladder inflammation) and even urinary blockages if they eat any kind of fish at all.

Fish and fish meal are both problematic. A small amount of fish, such as wild caught sardines, used as a flavouring in a properly balanced, fresh meat-based diet, is not a problem. But fish should not be the main course for the cat's diet.

But what about Omega 3 fatty acids? Aren't fish and fish oils the best sources

of these essential fats for our pets?

Indeed, daily Omega- 3 supplementation from a marine source is extremely important for our cats as well as for us. Among many other benefits, Omega 3s fight inflammation, which affects our cats as much as it does us. Krill is a popular non-fish source for Omega-3 oil. Krill are the major food source for many marine animals, including fish, whales, seals, and birds. Yes, there are a lot of krill in the sea, but the problem is that they are being harvested near critical feeding grounds of the animals that eat them. When even Whole Foods stops selling krill oil, as they did in 2010 due to concerns about sustainability, you know there's a problem!

Cats do benefit greatly from an Omega-3 marine lipid supplement every day, but as we have seen, fish and krill oils are not the most environmentally friendly choices. Nor are they necessarily healthful. Many fish oils are processed by boiling the oil to separate it from heavy metals and toxins (distillation). Fish oil processing may also include the use of, alcohol, salts, solvents, and deodorizers to disguise the foul smell of the oil—a problem because fish decompose very quickly, turning the oil rancid before it can even be processed. Additionally, as energy medicine practitioners, quantum physicians, and homeopaths know, the original energetic essence or "memory" of those heavy metals and pollutants, remains "imprinted" in the greasy substance that remains. The Omega 3s that survive, EPA and DHA, may be artificially concentrated in the process. It may be fair to say that the higher milligram values listed on fish oil labels are not necessarily better, as this is not the way they occur in their raw, natural state.

We need an alternative source of marine lipids for all these reasons, as well as the cautions mentioned for the eating of these fish. Research suggests that the New Zealand, greenlip mussel (perna canaliculus) is our best choice for Omega 3's. These greenlip mussels (GLM) are raised 100% sustainably. They are very low on the food chain; and have no fins, feet, or faces. GLM are bi-valve mollusks known to be a rich source of 33 fatty acids; 18 of them Omega 3s. GLM contain a unique array of Omega 3s. One of the most fascinating is ETA (eicosatetraenoic acid). ETA, which is not found in any other foods to any measurable degree, has extremely powerful ant-inflammatory properties. The best scenario is to source a greenlip mussel oil that is organic, cold-extracted, and certified to be free of mercury and other toxins and pollutants. Ideally, choose a GLM marine lipid product which also contains antioxidants with high ORAC values (a measure of antioxidant power), such as cold-pressed, organic grape seed husk extract and/or kiwifruit seed oil—these will naturally deactivate free radicals, as well as serve as natural preservatives for the GLM oil. While it doesn't affect quality, a common complaint about fish oil capsules is their size. They are enormous! GLM oil comes in tiny capsules that are perfect for cats, who will often eat them right from your hand; or they can be punctured and the contents mixed with wet food. Sources for quality Omega 3 greenlip mussel oil supplements are available online, and are proving to be the most beneficial and ecologically sound alternative to fish and krill oil.

www.paleodogbook.com

N.B. Celeste was suddenly diagnosed with Cancer at the end of last year and yet has not missed a beat when it comes to ensuring that our magazine had copy, even sending it from hospital in the middle of chemotherapy or post-op, please help her to cover the uninsured costs she and her husband need to find in order to get healthy again with as much natural treatment as possible via her gofundme page:

http://www.gofundme.com/kvo9xs

Thank You

Volume 2 Issue 3 September 2015

World Rabies Day—28th September

H B Turner

First written about in Mesopotamia in 1930 B.C. rabies has been around for 4,000 years. Whilst the first medical record of rabies in a human was registered in Boston in 1768 (Baer, 1991), there are many other forms of records. Early medieval records depict lycanthropy as does ancient Greek literature, one of the most famous of woodcutting depicts a 'werewolf' looking for all the world like a man gone mad.

In fact rabies is caused by *lyssaviruses* 'lyssa derived from the word 'lud' or 'violent', 'rabies' from the Latin meaning 'madness'.

Scratches or bites from an infected being spread the disease, causing acute inflammation of the brain leading to:-

- Violent movements
- Uncontrolled excitement
- Anxiety
- Agitation
- Paranoia
- Hallucinations
- Delirium
- Fear of water, also unquenchable thirst
- Inability to move parts of the body
- Confusion
- Loss of consciousness

Lucas Cranach the Elder 1512

Was this man bitten by a rabid animal?

Whilst the first stage of infection is characterised by behavioural changes, the second stage is known as "furious rabies", where the infected have a tendency to be hyper-reactive to external stimuli and bite anything in their immediate vicinity, it is obviously at this stage when others are most likely to also become infected. The third and final stage is paralytic, signs being drooling, difficulty swallowing, facial paralysis, limb paralysis and eventually respiratory arrest. Once the infected have passed, they will look simply as they had prior to infection (remind you of any myths?).

The UK has been rabies free since 1922 after imposing compulsory quarantine for dogs entering the country and introduced 'Pet Passports' in 2001, a number of other countries are also rabies free.

Whilst the pet passport system was first hailed as an invitation to bring Rabies into the country, it has so far proved efficacious. The system required however still entails a

Rabies free countries (in green) as of 2010)

wait. In order to qualify your pet (dog, cat or ferret), must be microchiped or tattood prior to being given a rabies vaccination, and for dogs a tapeworm treatment. Thirty days after the rabies vaccine your pet is required to have a blood test proving that the vaccine was successful, a copy of which you are required to keep to present to passport control, not until three months after this test can your pet travel. Unfortunately the required blood test does not always pass, and repeat vaccinations are often required, along with further waits prior to travel.

The first vaccine was developed by Louis Pasteur and Emile Roux in 1885 by taking nerve tissue from infected rabbits and allowing it to dry; another source of antibodies is consumption of infected birds after they have recovered (Gough & Jorgenson 1976, Jorgenson & Gough, 1976). Whilst rabies vaccines are not currently 100% efficacious (Murray *et al.* 2009), and have a number of side effects:-

- Immediate:
    - Vomiting
    - Facial Swelling
    - Fever
    - Lethargy
    - Circulatory Shock
    - Loss of consciousness
    - Death

- Delayed onset
    - Cancer at site of injection
    - Seizures or epilepsy
    - Autoimmune disease
    - Allergies
    - Skin diseases
    - Muscle weakness
    - Chronic digestive disorders
    - Behaviour issues
        (Jan Rasmusen—http://www.dogs4dogs.com/truth4dogs.html)

A new protocol of rabies vaccine manufacture has been identified as efficacious in all cases, this involves using membrane-anchored flagellin or Escherichia

N.B. We recommend reading Catherine O'Driscolls' 'Shock to the System' for more information on vaccine reactions, also please join her informative group via www.canine-health-concern.org.uk

coli in the vaccine (Qi *et al.* 2015) long term testing is still required. However current vaccines are detailed by the manufacturer as providing immunity from 1-4 years, but legal requirements are either annual or tri-annual vaccination in the United States. Results of a seven year research project (www.rabieschallengefund.org)by Prof. Ronald Schultz is expected to show at least 7 years of immunity from one vaccine, indicating yet more mandated over-vaccination (http://over-vaccination.net/questionable-vaccines/pet-vax/) leading to both short and long term side effects. Dr. Jeff Feinman has found successfully treated cases of vaccinosis from the Rabies Miasm (evidenced by behaviour changes) via the use of a homeopathic treatment used to treat Rabies (Feinman, 2015).

In exactly the same way as Cancer, Rabies requires an acidic environment and sugar (CDC , 2009) in order to replicate. If the history of lycantrophy is simply due to a lyssa virus contracted from a wild animal, or wolf with rabies, then it would make sense that these wolves were less afraid of people due to feeding on their refuse, taking in simple carbohydrates that are not species appropriate to their systems, hence leading them to have an acidic and sugar filled environment in which the rabies virus can successfully proliferate.

This being the case raw fed dogs on a species appropriate diet, containing no simple carbohydrates or sugars would be significantly less likely to contract this horrific, terminal disease.

References:

Baer, G.M. (1991) *The Natural History of Rabies.* 2nd Ed. CRC Press Inc. United States

CDC (2009) Rabies Post-Exposure Prophylaxis [Internet] Available from: http://www.cdc.gov/rabies/exposure/postexposure.html (Accessed 30/1/2010)

Feinman, J. (2015) How to Treat the Rabies Miasm. [Internet] Available from: http://certifiedvethomeopath.com/treat-rabies-miasm/?utm_campaign=coschedule&utm_source=facebook_page&utm_medium=Dogs%20Naturally%20Magazine (Accessed 01/05/2015)

Gough, P.M. Jorgenson, R.D. (1976) Rabies antibodies in sera of wild birds. *Journal of Wildlife Diseases* **12**[3]:392-395

Jorgenson, R.D. & Gough, P.M. (1976) Experimental rabies in a great horned owl. *Journal of Wildlife Diseases.* **12**[3]:444-447

Murray KO, Holmes KC, Hanlon CA. (2009) Rabies in vaccinated dogs and cats in the United States, 1997--2001. *J Am Vet Med Assoc* **235**:691--5

Qi, Y. Kang, H. Zheng, X. Wang, H. Gao, Y. Yang, S. & Xia, X. (2015) Incorporation of membrane-anchored flagellin or Escherichia Coli heat-labile enterotoxin B subunit enhances the immunogenicity of rabies virus-like particles in mice and dogs. *Frontiers in Microbiology.* [Internet] Available from: http://journal.frontiersin.org/Journal/10.3389/fmicb.2015.00169/pdf (Accessed 18/02/2015)

Genetic and Epigenetic Inheritance

H B Turner

Most people know that half of the genetics are inherited from the father and half from the mother, this makes up your genetic code or DNA i.e. the order of the acids in the chain. Whilst these do not change throughout life, individual genes and chains of genes can be 'turned' on or off through methylation or de-methylation this is termed epigenetics, and has been found to be sex specific.

Epigenetics can be influenced by stochastic events, such as trauma, but also through nutrition and environmental factors including stress, so whilst you or your pet may carry the genetics for diseases like particular types of cancer these genes may never be triggered, meaning removal of body parts as preventative measures may be a physical trauma not worth risking.

Were you aware that the ovum you developed from was grown in the womb of your grandmother and that as well as inheriting your mothers' immune system you also inherited hers?

Not only do we, other mammals and even plants inherit immunity and propensity for disease through DNA but recent studies have shown that behaviours are also inherited, such as maternal care.

How a mother brings up her young can be influence by how she in turn was raised, including the diet of her mother, environmental factors and even what compensatory measures her mother had to engage in to counterbalance any issues perceived with the fathers' genes, whether it be due to diet, cardio or lung issues.

Mice have been shown to eat more and make a higher maternal investment in the young of diet deprived males; interestingly enough they only did this when they perceived the genetic issue through pheromones and were not able to judge what compensation might be needed if artificially inseminated.

Other groups of mice were shown to have epigenetic memory within their mammary glands of pregnancy, leading to a higher proliferation of milk ducts in the second pregnancy due to 90% of DNA methylation in luminal cell types not re-methylating after the first offspring.

This leads us to believe that the body not only makes it easier to feed and care young from second pregnancies, but that there is a great deal we do not know about how DNA 'changes' throughout life.

Whilst we can tract and predict litter colours and propensity for disease in our un-naturally selected pets, it is no secret that most pedigree breeds, through tandem repeats of DNA over many generations of breeding and inbreeding for specific qualities, that many have breed specific health issues, and this is none more obvious within small populations of rare species in breeding programmes in Zoos.

We do know that humans can subconsciously identify genetic compatibility through pheromones, this research suggests that we are not alone in that ability; which poses the question that rather than human selection of animal breeding partners, perhaps many of these 'disease genes' could be bred out if we rather encouraged that natural selection that they would have had in the wild.

The Truth About Vaccines

Catherine O'Driscoll

The Immune System and Inflammation

I have always believed that if you can name something, it ceases to have power over you. Therefore it's always been important to me to not only have the name of a condition (like arthritis, for example), but also to name what arthritis actually is, and what is happening in the body to make the condition manifest. Once you know what is happening (a diagnosis), and why it is happening ... you can often find a way to stop it happening (a cure).

Inflammation is behind allergies, food sensitivities, autoimmunity, brain damage and cancer. In fact, inflammation is at the root of most of the conditions seen by vets and, indeed, GPs.

Scientists have spent decades looking at the intricacies of the immune system. They've examined the roles of B and T cells, found in the white blood cells and involved in protecting us from disease, and delved deeper to look at cytokines, T-helper (Th) cells, and other components of the immune system. They've found that some inflammatory (allergic and autoimmune) conditions are seen where a Th1 response is predominant, and others where Th2 is predominant.

Hashimoto's thyroiditis, multiple sclerosis, rheumatoid arthritis, Crohn's disease, Type 1 diabetes and psoriasis fall into the category of Th1 dominance, which means that there are more Th1 cells circulating around the body than Th2 cells.

Th1 cells act against pathogens (disease causing agents) that live and replicate inside our cells, such as viruses and some types of bacteria. So, if someone has a Th1 dominance within their immune system, you may be able to assume that their body is responding to a virus or bacteria that's embedded within their cells, but not necessarily manifesting as a viral or bacterial disease. They are chronically infected.

In contrast, Graves' disease, asthma, lupus, and seasonal allergies are associated with a predominance of Th2 cells. Th2 cells are found outside of cells in body fluids. This pathway becomes activated in the presence of parasites and some types of bacteria, and there is also an upregulation of Th2 dominance associated with vaccination.

For example, many autoimmune and atopic conditions are associated with an over-representation of Th2 cells, which is related to antibody production. Hashimoto's thyroiditis, on the other hand (which is nevertheless an autoimmune disease) shows a predominance of Th1 cells. However, Hashimoto patients can also present with a mix of Th1 and Th2 dominance, and also with no clearly defined dominance.

Therefore it's not always clear whether, as scientists had hoped, a particular condition can be helped by stimulating the opposite Th response. Wouldn't it be wonderful if you could say ... "ah, Hashimoto's ... we need to upregulate Th2 cells". This could be done easily, with the aid of simple foodstuffs like curcumin from turmeric, green tea extract, or white willow bark.

If, on the other hand, you're treating a condition that's Th2 dominant, you could stimulate the opposite – Th1 cells – by giving chlorella, spirulina, Echinacea, selenium or panax ginseng.

Scientists thought that by identifying which inflammatory conditions related to which subset of Th cells, they could come up with effective and remarkably simple cures. But now they're realising that it's not as uniform as they had hoped, and that exceptions are proving the rule. In short, there is more to it than the immune system workers, or components, have been able to tell us.

New Information: The Vagus Nerve

Dr Kevin Tracey, a neurosurgeon based in New York, has discovered that there is a sort of CEO in the body that tells the immune system (the little workers called B and T cells, cytokines, Th cells, and so on) to jump into action, and to stand down.

Dr Tracey has hit upon the theory that the nervous system, particularly the vagus nerve, can tell the spleen to switch off inflammation everywhere in the body. If correct, inflammation in body tissues is being directly regulated by the brain. *The immune system is just carrying out the brain's wishes!*

Dr Tracey's discovery appears to be bringing together what is already known in psychoneuroimmunology (the study of the mind and emotions as they impact the immune system), and the body-mind movement.

In humans and other animals, the vagus nerve starts in the brainstem, just behind the ears. It travels down each side of the neck, across the chest and down through the abdomen. This bundle of nerve fibres roves through the body, networking the brain with the stomach and digestive tract, the lungs, heart, spleen, intestines, liver and kidneys, plus a range of other nerves that are involved in speech, eye contact, facial expressions and even your ability to tune in to other people's voices.

The vagus nerve is made of thousands and thousands of fibres and 80 per cent of them are sensory, meaning that the vagus nerve reports back to your brain what is going on in your organs.

Operating below the level of the conscious mind, the vagus nerve is vital for keeping our bodies healthy. It's an essential part of the parasympathetic nervous system, which is responsible for calming organs after the stressed 'fight-or-flight' adrenaline response to danger. Not all vagus nerves are the same, however: some people have stronger vagus activity, which means their bodies can relax faster after a stress.

It could be as simple as this for our dogs. Those who are very sensitive or highly strung – the ones we tend to have a really close connection with – are perhaps less able to regulate their immune systems. And maybe this is why it's always the 'one-in-a-million' dog who succumbs to immune-mediated disease.

Research shows that a high vagal tone makes your body better at regulating blood glucose levels, reducing the likelihood of diabetes, stroke, and cardiovascular disease. Low vagal tone, however, has been associated with chronic inflammation.

One of the vagus nerve's jobs is to reset the immune system and switch off production of proteins that fuel inflammation. Low vagal tone means this regulation is less effective and inflammation can become excessive

Having found evidence of a role for the vagus in a range of chronic inflammatory diseases, including rheumatoid arthritis, Tracey and his colleagues wanted to see if it could become a possible route for treatment. The vagus nerve works as a two-way messenger, passing electrochemical signals between the organs and the brain.

In chronic inflammatory disease, Tracey figured, messages from the brain telling the spleen to switch off production of a particular inflammatory protein, tumour necrosis factor (TNF), weren't being sent. Perhaps the signals could be boosted?

He spent the next decade mapping all the neural pathways involved in regulating TNF, from the brainstem to the mitochondria inside cells.

Tracey then developed an electronic device, similar to a pacemaker, to stimulate the vagus nerve. More than a thousand people expressed interest in the procedure and trials went ahead.

The results are still being prepared for publication but more than half of the patients showed significant improvement and around one-third are in remission – in effect cured of their rheumatoid arthritis. Sixteen of the 20 patients on the trial not only felt better, but measures of inflammation in their blood also went down. Some are now entirely drug-free. Even those who have not experienced clinically significant improvements with the implant insist it helps them; nobody wants it removed.

The technique has proved so successful – and so appealing to patients – that other researchers are now looking into using vagal nerve stimulation for a range of other chronic debilitating conditions, including inflammatory bowel disease, asthma, diabetes, chronic fatigue syndrome and obesity.

The Mind-Body connection

Low vagal tone is associated with a range of health risks, whereas people with high vagal tone are healthier and also socially and psychologically stronger – better able to concentrate and remember things, happier and less likely to be depressed, more empathic and more likely to have close friendships.

Twin studies show that to a certain extent, vagal tone is genetically predetermined – some people are born luckier than others. But low vagal tone is more prevalent in those with certain lifestyles – people who do little exercise, for example. This led psychologists at the University of North Carolina to wonder if the relationship between vagal tone and wellbeing could be harnessed without the need for implants.

In 2010, Barbara Fredrickson and Bethany Kok recruited around 70 university staff members for an experiment. Each volunteer was asked to record the strength of emotions they felt every day. Vagal tone was measured at the beginning of the experiment and at the end, nine weeks later. As part of the experiment, half of the participants were taught a meditation technique to promote feelings of goodwill towards themselves and others.

Those who meditated showed a significant rise in vagal tone, which was associated with reported increases in positive emotions. "That was the first experimental evidence that if you increased positive emotions and that led to increased social closeness, then vagal tone changed," Kok says.

Now at the Max Planck Institute in Germany, Kok is conducting a much larger trial to see if the results they found can be replicated. If so, vagal tone could one day be used as a diagnostic tool. In a way, it already is. "Hospitals already track heart-rate variability – vagal tone – in patients that have had a heart attack," she says, "because it is known that having low variability is a risk factor."

The implications of being able to simply and cheaply improve vagal tone, and so relieve immune-mediated diseases, are enormous. It has the potential to completely change how we view disease.

Modulating the Vagus Nerve

It's very easy for humans to get the body, and particularly the vagus nerve, to work with them. How we do it for our dogs is another matter – but I

think it can be done, simply because our dogs are so in tune with us that if we are calm and happy, our dogs will be too.

In many cultures, breath (qi, chi, prana) is considered the vital link to energy, awareness and composure. How we breathe is now being linked to our health.

Research has found that proper breathing can improve heart rate variability and reduce immune activation.

When you stimulate your vagus nerve through mindful breathing, you counteract your sympathetic nervous system, the one that causes stress by activating the fight-or-flight response.

There are three types of breathing:

Clavicular breathing — a breath that comes from high up in the shoulders and collarbones

Chest breathing — a breath that comes from the centre of the chest

Abdominal breathing — a breath that comes from the abdomen

The third kind of breath is the one we need to practice if we wish to boost our health. It comes from the abdomen and uses the diaphragm. When the diaphragm contracts, your lungs expand, pulling air in through your mouth like bellows. When you breathe from your abdomen, your belly will expand and move out with each inhalation. Your chest will rise slightly, but not nearly as much as with chest breathing; your abdomen is doing all the moving.

Doing abdominal breathing, you can activate the vagus nerve and trigger a relaxation response. The relaxation response, which is the opposite of the stress response, is necessary for the body to heal, repair, and renew.

One technique to stimulate the vagus nerve through breathing is called the 4-7-8 technique. Here, you breathe in through your nose, to your diaphragm, for a count of four. Then hold for seven. Then breathe out through your mouth to a count of eight. Do this from six to twelve times. You'll feel an incredible sense of relaxation. And not only that – you'll be sending messages to your over-active immune system to get out of the flight-fight response, and relax.

Have your dog sitting with you and keep him in mind as you do this exercise. As one police dog handler said to me: "The dog's temperament travels down the lead."

Stimulating your vagus nerve controls the parasympathetic nervous system. Researchers have discovered that 'acetylcholine' is released by the vagus nerve. This neurotransmitter not only relaxes you, but it also turns down the fires of inflammation.

Exciting new research has also linked the vagus nerve to improved neurogenesis (the growth and development of nervous tissue), increased BDNF output (brain-derived neurotrophic factor is like super fertilizer for your brain cells) and repair of brain tissue, and to regeneration throughout the body.

Stems cells are also directly connected to the vagus nerve. Activating the vagus nerve can stimulate stem cells to produce new cells and repair and rebuild organs.

Have Vaccines Spread Distemper to Other Species?

Distemper used to be the most serious viral disease affecting dogs. A relative of the measles virus, canine distemper didn't have its first recorded case described until 1905, although it first appeared in Europe in 1761.

The first distemper vaccine was developed in 1923, with a commercial vaccine being developed in 1950. In the early 1980s, post-vaccine encephalitis (brain and central nervous system damage) was reported in dogs from various parts of Britain after administration of a particular batch of combined Rockborn strain distemper/canine adenovirus type-1 vaccine. This, and other reports, led to the view that the Rockborn strain is less safe than other distemper vaccines, and the Rockborn strain was officially withdrawn from the markets in the mid- 1990s.

However, in 2010, Rockborn-like strains were identified in two vaccines currently in the market. These findings indicate that Rockborn-like viruses may be recovered from dogs or other carnivores with distemper, suggesting cases of residual virulence of vaccines, or circulation of vaccine-derived Rockborn-like viruses in the field. Expressed less technically, distemper was being spread in dogs and other meat-eaters by the vaccine designed to prevent it.

The domestic dog has been blamed for introducing canine distemper to previously unexposed wildlife, "causing a serious conservation threat to many species of carnivores and some species of marsupials. The virus contributed to the near-extinction of the black-footed ferret. It also may have played a considerable role in the extinction of the Tasmanian tiger and recurrently causes mortality among African wild dogs. In 1991, the lion population in Serengeti, Tanzania, experienced a 20% decline as a result of the disease. The disease has also mutated to form phocid distemper virus, which affects seals."

The biologist Roger Burrows was studying wild dogs in Africa when a mass vaccination programme was initiated amongst wild dogs. He tells me that it was only after the vaccine was administered that wild dogs started to die. He feels that the vaccine created the problem.

What is rarely admitted is the fact that distemper vaccines were more likely to have caused these wildlife disasters than dogs – due to vaccine-derived Rockborn-like viruses being injected into dogs and then shed through their faeces and infecting other species.

(Lights and shades on an historical vaccine canine distemper virus, the Rockborn strain - ResearchGate. Available from: http:// www.researchgate.net/.../49691867_Lights_and_shades_on... [accessed Jul 14, 2015].)

www.canine-health-concern.org.uk

Canine Health Concern

Nick Thompson

NICK THOMPSON

CANINE NUTRITION
Hypothyroidism & Vaccinations

brought to you by

holisticvet

RAW DOG FOOD
WWW.RAWDOGFOOD.CO/SEMINARS

We are thrilled to be able to bring you this new video series by the incredible Nick Thompson.

Canine Nutrition, Hypothyroidism and Vaccinations features over five hours worth of video covering the following subjects.

An introduction to Raw Food for Dogs.

Why consider changing from tins or kibble?

- How safe and complete are raw foods?
- How to choose a ready made raw food
- How to make your own raw food diet

Hypothyroidism, Behaviour, Epilepsy & Chronic Disease.

- 43% of English Setters have Autoimmune Thyroiditis
- Golden Retriever, Cocker Spaniel, Boxer and Labrador breeds are all in the top 25 most commonly affected breeds
- Groups at higher risk for behavioural disorders due to thyroid disease include. pedigrees, neutered males and females and mid to large sized dogs

Vaccination in the 21st Century.

- Why "re-starting" vaccines is "inconsistent" with the principles of immunological memory
- Why blood testing (titre testing) is the future
- When to titre test
- When to vaccinate puppies; when not to
- When to vaccinate old dogs; when not to
- How useful is Kennel Cough Vaccine

We think this is a complete bargain at only £24.99.

Click **here** for access or go to http://t.co/WvKTa1WUGt

Recommended Reading

Canine Nutrigenomics	Dodds, J.W. & Laverdure, D.R
Food Pets Die For	Ann N. Martin
Heal Your Dog the Natural Way	Richard Allport
Natural Healthcare for Pets	Richard Allport
Paleo Dog	Jean Hofve & Celeste Yarnall
Pottenger's Cats	Francis M. Pottenger
Raw Meaty Bones	Tom Lonsdale
Shock to the System	Catherine O'Driscoll
Ten Top Tips on Reducing the Cost of Raw Feeding	H B Turner
The BARF Diet	Dr Ian Billinghurst
The Complete Herbal Handbook for the Dog and Cat	Juliette de Baïracli Levy
The Healthful Dog Blog	H B Turner
The Homeopathic Treatment of Small Animals	Christopher Day
The Natural Rearing Breeder	H B Turner
The Science Behind Canine Raw Feeding	H B Turner
The Science of Homoeopathy	George Vithoulkas
Unlock Your Dog's Potential	Sarah Fisher
What Vets Don't Tell you about Vaccines	Catherine O'Driscoll

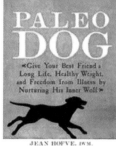

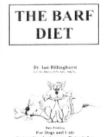
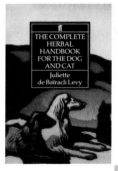
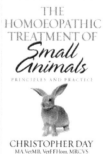

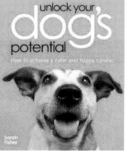

Recommended Resources

Amazon	www.amazon.co.uk/.com
American Homeopathic Veterinary Medical Association	www.ahvma.org
Association of Non-Veterinary Natural Animal Health Practitioners	www.annahp.co.uk
Australian Association of Holistic Veterinarians	www.aha.com.au
British Association of Homeopathic Veterinary Surgeons	www.bahvs.com
Canine Health Concern (CHC)	www.canine-health-concern.org.uk
Chip Me Not	www.ChipMeNot.org
Complementary Veterinary Medicine Group of the South African Veterinary Association	www.cvmg.co.za
DEFRA	www.defra.gov.uk
Merck Veterinary Manual	www.merckmanuals.com/vet
Price Pottenger Nutrition Foundation (PPNF)	www.ppnf.org
Raw Food Vets	www.rawfoodvets.com
Royal College of Veterinary Surgeons	www.rcvs.org.uk
VacciCheck Vets	www.petwelfarealliance.org/vaccicheck.html
Veterinary Medical Directorate	www.vmd.defra.gov.uk
Worm Count Lab	www.wormcount.com
World Small Animal Veterinary Association	www.WSAVA.org

"It's not a statistic when it's your pet."

Healthful Dog Journalzine is sponsored by ANNAHP and Wagdale & published by Talen Publications

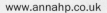

www.annahp.co.uk | www.wagdale.org.uk | facebook.com/TalenPublications

Printed in Great Britain
by Amazon